WALLACE NUTTING

Supreme Edition

GENERAL CATALOG

Schiffer Limited

EXTON, PENNSYLVANIA 19341

CONTENTS—INDEX

Andirons	149–152	Hat Racks	30, 90
Beds	7	Highboys	45
Benches	21, 24	Office Furniture (adapted)	140
Books	139	Iron Utensils	147
Boxes	60, 61	Lectures	139
Brasses	158, 151, 155	Lighting Fixtures	147, 150, 153
Calendars	138	Mirrors	128
Candlestands	120	Pictures	134
Chairs, mahogany	63	Pipe Boxes	21
Chairs, maple	75	Rooms	7, 15, 23, 26, 41, 89, 99, 116
Chairs, walnut	71, 74	Rugs	37, 41, 55, 138
Chairs, wing	70, 91	Screens	20, 71
Chaise Longue	7, 9, 19	Secretaries	36
Chests	59	Settees	92
Chests of drawers, low	52	Settings, see rooms	
Chests of drawers, high	45	Settles	91, 92
Chest-on-chest	50	Shelves	29
Chest-on-frame	56	Sideboards	113, 114
Clocks	124, 44	Sideboard Tables	106, 112, 114
Commercial	140	Signs	56
Crib	16	Small Articles, see Wooden Ware	
Cupboards	27, 43	Sofas	96, 98
Day Beds	7, 9, 19	Spoon Rack	21
Desks	36	Stands	20, 120, 128
Dressers	30	Stools	22, 54, 128
Dumb Waiter	43	Tables	99
Glasses	128	Window Seat	21
Finials	39, 95	Wooden Ware	14, 34, 57, 62, 109

Wallace Nutting General Catalog, Supreme Edition

Originally published by Wallace Nutting, Framingham, Massachusetts, 1930

This reprint edition, with corrections and additions, copyright © 1977, Schiffer Limited, Box E. Exton, Pennsylvania 19341.

Library of Congress catalog card number: 77-608284
ISBN: 0-916838-09-9

Manufactured in the United States of America

Do you own a "Wallace Nutting"?

Besides writing *The Furniture Treasury*, Wallace Nutting operated a large factory in the early decades of this century, making high quality furniture reproductions, many very similar to the antiques pictured in *The Furniture Treasury*. This is his catalog. It will be both fascinating and disturbing.

Many young collectors, dealers, auctioneers and appraisers could not have seen this catalog which has been out of print and for all practical purposes unavailable for over thirty years. For them this book is essential.

We, in the Herbert Schiffer Antiques appraisal service, sometimes have the distressing duty to inform people that a treasured heirloom is actually a Nutting reproduction. This job is increasingly more difficult for these pieces now have fifty years of age and wear. Occasionally unscrupulous people have accelerated this aging process, increasing the need for accurate identification by a competent appraiser.

If this book prevents one such mistake, it will be worthwhile reading. Nutting furniture is being collected in it's own right today, and this book is the only guide.

As publishers, we are interested in making available new books that will be of enduring value in the decorative arts field. We are equally desirous to reprint books of proven merit.

SCHIFFER LIMITED
Exton, Pa. 19341

Wallace Nutting

is a professional man turned out to grass by the
doctors a long time ago. He surprised them by a
recovery which however required some years.

Born at Rockbottom, Massachusetts, in 1861, he
was reared in Maine, and educated at the Augusta
High School, at Phillips Exeter Academy, New
Hampshire, at Harvard College, at Hartford Seminary, and Union Seminary, New York. He served
churches in Newark, in St. Paul, in Seattle and in
Providence.

A good number of summers were spent in Vermont,
several winters in Florida and California. Thus
by residence or training he has had a year or more
in ten states, and by travel has pictured most of
the other states, and in part ten foreign lands.

When driven out of doors he began to consider

what contribution would be most valuable in his power to American history. This led him to picture the beauties of our beloved land, first out of doors, and later in doors, until he accumulated many thousands of illustrations, with special reference to the early life and occupations of our fathers, and their environment,—their dwellings and furniture, their gardens and orchards, their winding old roads and farm streams. The record comprises a hundred or more familiar occupations in still more numerous backgrounds of our mothers and fathers.

This absorbing, and one may hope, really valuable record has extended over most of the states and has here and there reached not a few foreign lands.

The production of orchard and garden and "Colonial" platinotypes in hand color has been stated, we suppose correctly, to have originated with Dr. Nutting. These pictures are on the walls, literally, of many millions of American homes.

As time went on it was seen to be desirable to gather these records in volumes. The result has been about twenty books. Some of the States Beautiful Series reach editions of thirty thousand each, and each contains above three hundred illustrations, with description. Asked why no second edition ever appears he explains the process by which these pictures are reproduced requires large editions so that a thousand or so extra copies cannot practically be supplied. He is therefore now engaged in producing not only volumes on states hitherto omitted, but also on two states to produce wholly new matter for a second setting forth.

But side by side with this occupation has gone on the study of the interiors and decorations of our old homes, until a dozen have been restored as monuments and conveyed to various organizations. In this process six books on early furniture have been produced, the last of which, with its two large volumes, contains no less than 5000 pictures.

In this joyful but exacting occupation the collections of Dr. Nutting have been used as backgrounds for old fashioned studies. The extensive collection of the Pilgrim century period was acquired by the Hartford Atheneum, by the munificent gift of the present J. P. Morgan. There it is visited freely by all.

In this study, in order to know the whole truth about furnishings, a great number of old pieces were taken apart, inspected and repaired. Requests for copies of unique or quaint or beautiful specimens led

to the establishment of a complete shop for reproductions, where hundreds of patterns from the simplest to the richest have been produced. While this
work has never been profitable financially, it has
compelled an absolutely strict attention to the de-
tails of old forms and has been an education on these
lines of the highest value, not only for Dr. Nutting
but all associated with him. All are schooled to
follow the solid original processes, to avoid the shoddy
and to work irrespective of time required. One of
the ten commandments in the shop is "never let a
piece of work leave your hands till you are proud
of it."

A generation since a collection and study was made
of the wrought iron utensils and applied hardware of
early houses. This also is produced in every good
form. We believe the Nutting forge has shown
fifteen hundred patterns. It avoids all bizarre style.

In order to make the results available in another
way, about three thousand colored slides have been
made for illustration before clubs, schools and
societies, covered by twenty-five lectures, of which
there is a prospectus.

Not a little has been done by way of consultation
regarding the reproduction of very early houses and
interior backgrounds. Mrs. Nutting has produced
exquisite patterns of drawn in (hooked rugs) but in
the largest sizes only, since small rugs are everywhere
available. Many persons have become skilful in
helping on these matters. Some have been twenty
years in the studio or shop. Lately, Mr. Ernest John
Donnelly, the secretary, and far more than a secretary, has produced a large and fascinating list of
silhouettes of a very high order.

The headquarters at Framingham, half way from
Boston to Worcester, on the main railways and the
new trunk line highway, are visited continually from
every quarter and are open to all, every week day
including Saturday. This visitation has been said
by several judges of national repute to afford a range
of interest in the examination of the productions,
which leaves a recollection of red letter days to all
who love beauty.

In fact these headquarters not only delight the
casual guest but are a storehouse of books, furniture,
fixtures, and illustrations. The drives are beautiful;
excellent over-night quarters accessible, and all
elements contribute to make a stay of several
days agreeable, so near the sources of the best of the
earlier features of American life.

WALLACE NUTTING
Furniture

Central in New England. Half way from Boston to Worcester. Six main motor spokes meet here, from Providence, the Cape, the mountains, the North Shore, the Berkshires and the West, New York and Maine. Wellesley and Newton are our close eastern neighbors, and the Sudbury Wayside Inn to the north, then Concord.

We are close to the Framingham station (see name on shop north from train). Express trains from New York and the West and Boston. A good hotel a block away. Many people spend the night here, or near here, then all day studying the unprecedentedly large display of early furniture styles.

There are superb drives in several directions. Our visitors come from everywhere, and our customers from all the states, Canada and Europe.

The new motor route from Hartford through Stafford Springs is short and all rural.

We have become the advisers of thoughtful, well-bred people on furnishings.

INVESTMENTS THAT COUNT

A broker whose office was furnished by me said he believed the prestige derived from the equipment of his office would pay for it in three months. Anyhow, he died rich.

Persons furnishing homes are not in the habit of doing so to enhance their fortunes. But it is a bald fact that the value of my furniture increases faster than most good investments. And while this is going on the furniture is a continual source of satisfaction, a pride, a comfort and a distinction. I am getting elderly. Shrewd business men have told me that pieces bearing my name will soon be coveted by collectors. The thought did not originate with me. Think it over.

WHY SHOP AROUND?

Persons in every station can come here and if they are not beyond taking advice, can be provided, at modest prices, with everything, absolutely, needed in a home, except affection, and even that will be less likely to fly out of the window, when their children arise up and call them blessed for getting decorations that become constantly more beautiful and valuable.

OLD OR NEW FURNITURE?

A child's high chair made by me, and sold as new for nineteen dollars, was artificially aged and resold for a cool thousand. Nobody but the maker could have discovered the imposition.

There lies now in a pigeon hole in my office an offer from a large English firm to supply anything I want with the guarantee that it will not be discovered to be spurious. Thus even museums have been hoaxed, and the public are buying new furniture and paying ten prices for it. The only available expert is a dealer. Will he consent to enter another's shop and pronounce on forgeries? He has better business. One of the keenest, most experienced judges in America states that practically all furniture imported from southern Europe is new, and nearly all from northern Europe. A recent buyer returned from England and advertised that he had brought with him "a thousand pieces of Duncan Phyfe"! And for that matter it was as much so as most that passes under that name.

THE STYLE IS THE THING

This being so, some people rather than pay forty-four thousand for a piece of furniture, the styles of the top and bottom of which do not, even at that price, agree, have recognized that the style and the construction are the main items.

The sweet flowing curves and soft colors of real reproductions give the atmosphere, the charm, the sentiment, the dignity of the old. Trade furniture was shown me recently with spurious pins, without tenons under them. Its sales are vast. Disgust with such widespread enacted lies has induced me to open my shop to customers who can see the work go together — big tenons into big mortises. The dowel is the bane of furniture. To begin with, it makes construction only one quarter as expensive. It is weak from the first, rickety shortly, a disgrace to the maker, a sorrow and shame to the owner, the shoddy symbol of a shoddy age.

People of education like stylish and solid furniture. Such furniture gives a background to life, and will last hundreds of years and grow in value every year.

THE ANTIQUE OF THE FUTURE

My furniture, when homes have broken up, is never sold as second hand. In all instances that have come to my attention, it has brought more than was paid for it! Wide-awake persons now know that my name branded on furniture means style and quality. I bow humbly to certain noble and wise men whose knowledge is far greater than mine. But back of this furniture is the fullest work on the subject, extending to five thousand pictures and 1536 pages, the "Furniture Treasury," the tearing apart of old furniture for twenty years, and the knowledge, on the part of my friends, that I have expended a moderate fortune in recreating five hundred types, as worthy as care can make them, of all good periods including mahogany.

SCOPE

Five rooms can be furnished, simply but soundly, for eight hundred dollars. Or ten rooms can be furnished rather magnificently with rich dignity for twenty thousand dollars. Some of the old types of chairs are so comfortable that our customers here fall asleep blissfully and wake to ecstasy.

WHEN OPEN

Every week day including Saturday, till six o'clock, and also on holidays except Thanksgiving and Christmas. Phone — Framingham 1326.

My residence, not open to the public, is at Framingham Center, on the Common, at 24 Vernon Street, two miles from the shop. Phone 782.

THE WALLACE NUTTING COLLECTION

By the gift of Mr. J. Pierpont Morgan, my collection is in the Atheneum, Hartford. No, I no longer buy antiques, not even Paisley shawls.

THE SOURCE OF MY COPIES ARE

1. The Wallace Nutting Collection at Hartford.
2. The former collection, with much mahogany.
3. The collections of the Metropolitan Museum, of which I have the honor of being a member.
4. The collections of many friends who have been kind enough to give me access for measurements.

I would gladly include their names here, were it not for the resulting embarrassment to them. They are among the best collectors in the country. They include some thirty persons. Thus the range is extremely broad, the types and periods complete and satisfactory.

THE UPHOLSTERY DEPARTMENT

In order to ensure the quality of the upholstery, and to know absolutely what enters into it, I have added that work to my shop. Customers may see for themselves the quality. The use of down, in part, for the loose cushions, the use of pigskin where ordered, are thus no longer a matter of anxiety.

In fact the cutting, turning, joining, carving, finishing, rush seating, upholstery are all done under one roof and to people who like to watch good construction it affords great satisfaction.

BEDS

A variety of fifty styles of beds is offered, and is believed to cover every demand from the canopied high poster to the very low popular "hired man's" bed.

These beds are all made in the old manner with mortised posts, and held together by bolts. The construction, while involving greater labor, produces a permanently good bed, always graceful and emphatically reminiscent of the olden time.

As a rule the style follows the mid-eighteenth century low bed rail, to allow for an upholstered spring, nine inches deep, built so that four inches is below, and five inches above the rail. The upper part extends out over the full width of the rail, to give width, comfort and a good appearance. The spring therefore must be built with a cut out corner to fit about the post. We supply these springs at very slight additional cost, and always with complete satisfaction to the customer. We also supply the high grade hair mattress with the cut out corner, at no additional expense. See the price list at close of catalog, beginning with No. 801, for sizes and qualities. A somewhat poorer quality of hair may be used but we do not advise it. Ordinary modern springs may easily be adapted for the beds, but we do not attempt that work. The headboards appear high because the spring and mattress require it.

Customers will please be careful in ordering beds to specify sizes. Otherwise we cannot be responsible. The sizes given are all outside, and the mattress is the same size, not smaller. It is merely necessary to write "single," "narrow double," or "wide double" unless some special size is required. Beds are all 82 in. long. The single is 39 in. wide; the narrow double is 54 in. and the wide double is 60 in. wide.

The charge for a double bed of any width is uniformly four dollars more than the single. No charge for a special size; it will be billed at the price of a double bed. All beds are sold double except Nos. 811, 812, 834 and 849, and we advise against 836 as double, it being more slender. No. 834 is under single size.

We do not wish to be responsible for the curl of maple posts larger than two inches, as it may not satisfy the customers. The rails even of mahogany beds are stained maple, as they never show, except the rich Nos. 806, 840 and 841 which have rails of mahogany with an edge mold. Headboards of walnut and mahogany and maple beds are of the same wood as the bed, except that 807, 808 and 809 have one piece pine headboards.

Single beds have the end sections built as a unit and pinned permanently, only the side rail taking down. Double beds knock down completely. Thus there are only four bolts in a single, and eight in a double bed. Bolt caps accompany all beds gratis. We never use casters, but heavy domes of silence which are more satisfactory, injuring the floor less, sliding more easily and not interfering with the antique type.

828 MAPLE OR WALNUT. EIGHT LEG DAY BED. SWING HEAD
23 X 70 X 30 HIGH. RUSH SEAT

A ROOM EVERY ARTICLE OF WHICH IS MADE IN OUR SHOP

846B MAHOGANY (MAPLE ONLY TO ORDER). REEDED, SHERATON,
67 HIGH

809   LOW, URN POST. MAPLE,
38 HIGH

842   PERIOD 1830. FOOT RAIL,
$52\frac{1}{2}$ HIGH

829   EIGHT LEG, WALNUT DAY BED, SWING HEAD, $39\frac{3}{4}$ X 23 X 71

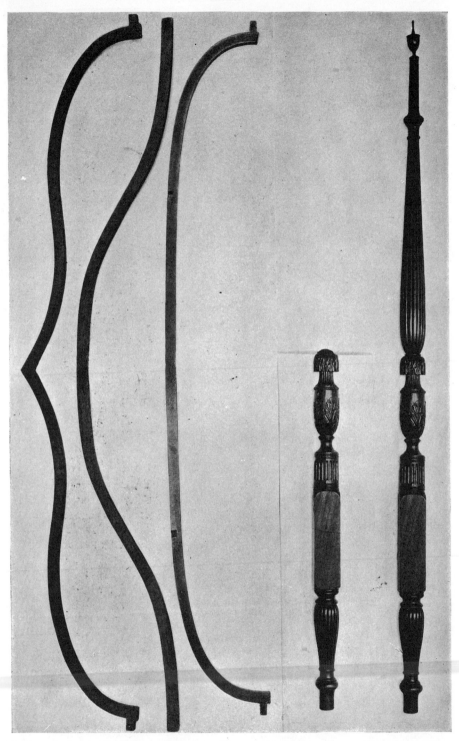

826 HIGH SHERATON, MAHOGANY, 88 HIGH. 826B HALF HIGH, 45 HIGH
CANOPY FRAME SHAPES. 819 PLAIN OVAL. 820 PLAIN OGEE.
818B POINTED OGEE

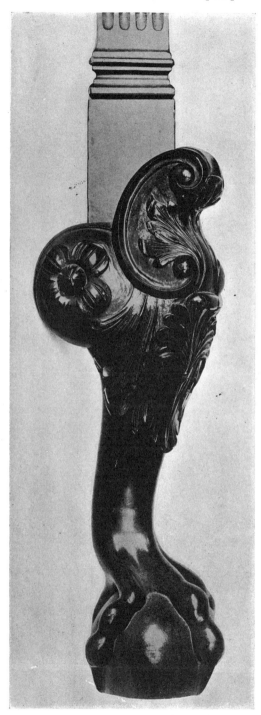

806   MAHOGANY. SQUARE FLUTED
POST, RICH, EFFECTIVE CHIP-
PENDALE, 83 HIGH

841   CHIP. CLUSTERED COL-
UMN. TWO OR FOUR
CARVED POSTS

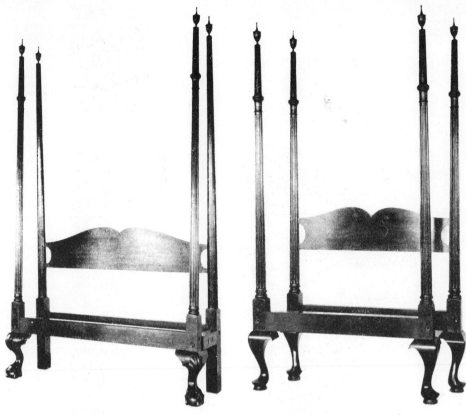

840 MAHOGANY, 82 HIGH
BEST CHIPPENDALE SCHOOL

845 WALNUT, 76 HIGH
QUEEN ANNE TYPE

In the ball and claw foot bed above the post is made of one piece, four inches square, heavy mahogany, and not pieced as in commercial beds. Only the bracket is attached. The rails have a dainty inset quarter round mold, and are of solid mahogany. For still finer beds see page 11. 841, however, is square below the rail and molded.

845 above has a solid walnut post of one piece of wood. It is also supplied with the foot posts only shaped.

834 N. Y. BED, 71 X 26 X 30. 849 SAME, 42 HIGH,
REGULAR SINGLE SIZE

807   POSTS, $2\frac{3}{8}$ X $44\frac{1}{2}$ FOOT POSTS, 38 HIGH, MAPLE

808   POSTS, $2\frac{3}{8}$ X 38, FOOT, $28\frac{1}{2}$ MAPLE

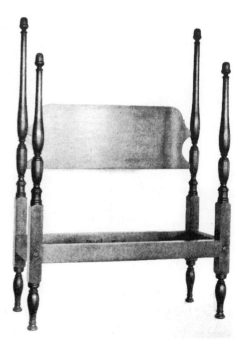

836   LIGHT AND DAINTY, CURLY PLAIN IF DESIRED. $60\frac{1}{2}$ HIGH

847   HALF HIGH, ACORN. MAPLE, 56 HIGH. MAHOGANY TO ORDER

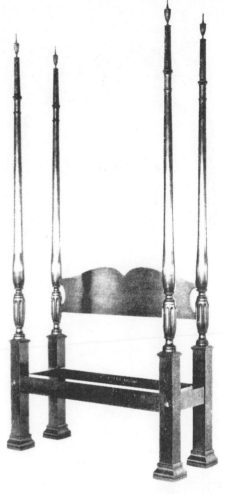

848 HEPPLEWHITE, TAPER REEDED
POST 76 HIGH, MAHOGANY OR
MAPLE. SINGLE OR DOUBLE

827 CARVED, MAPLE, 82 HIGH,
82 LONG
MADE ALSO IN MAHOGANY TO ORDER

CURLY TRENCHERS, SALTS, AND TRAYS. UNIQUE AND BEAUTIFUL.
PRACTICAL. 30B LEFT; 30 MIDDLE; 26 RIGHT; 27 LARGE
SALT; 28 SMALL SALT; 29 TRAY

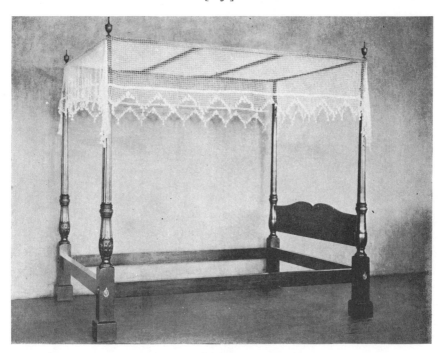

832 CARVED MAHOGANY. 832B SAME, FOUR POSTS CARVED. CANOPY EXTRA, 83 HIGH

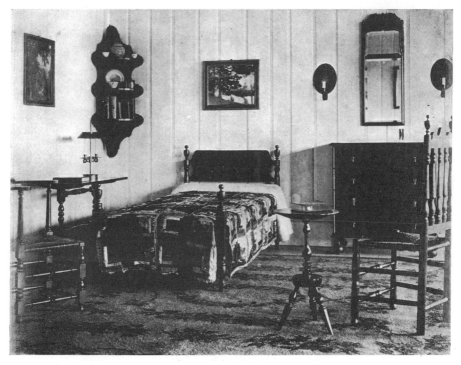

MAPLE ROOM SO CALLED. EVERYTHING SHOWN INCLUDING RUG MADE BY US

810 CHILD'S WALNUT CRIB. DAINTY UNIQUE
PATTERN. 47 HIGH, 43 LONG, 23 WIDE

821B SPADE FOOT, HEPPLEWHITE, REEDED URN, 75
HIGH. SINGLE OR DOUBLE. MAHOGANY OR MAPLE

846 MAPLE OR MAHOGANY, ANY SIZE, 66½ HIGH, OR WITH TESTER
THE MOST ATTRACTIVE SIMPLE SHERATON BED. SEE
ALSO PICTURE PAGE 8

839 PLAIN MAPLE, 55½ HIGH
839A POSTS, 2⅜ X 45

811 OAK OR MAPLE
ALL STYLES DOUBLE BEDS, 60 X 82

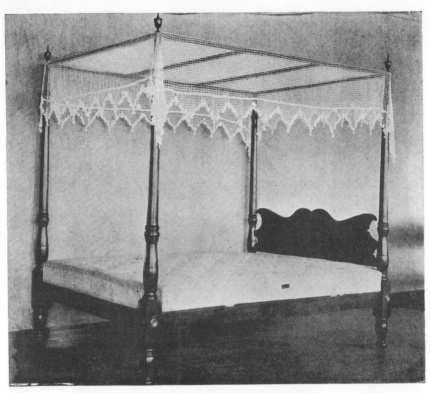

813   MAPLE, DOUBLE OR SINGLE

844   CURLY, DOUBLE OR SINGLE, 76½ HIGH

811

812 BREWSTER, 56 HIGH, AN ANCIENT PATTERN
TWO THIRDS SIZE, 42 IN. ONLY

825 MAPLE, 23 X 70, HEAD 30 HIGH

36   POLE SCREEN, BALL AND CLAW FOOT, CARVED HIP AND STANDARD.
SOLD WITH OR WITHOUT THE DECORATION ON THE SCREEN PROPER. THE
BOARD MAY BE MADE OF ANY SIZE, AND LONG VERTICALLY OR HORIZONTALLY,
BUT IT MUST BE RECTANGULAR. MAHOGANY. A VERY RICH ARTICLE. 51
INCHES HIGH

630   CARVED TORCHERE. BALL AND CLAW FEET, DROP BENEATH THE
STANDARD WHICH IS FLUTED IN A TRIANGULAR FORM AND THE FILLETS
SEEN UPON IT ARE CUT BY HAND. CIRCULAR TOP IS DISHED. MAHOGANY. $35\frac{1}{4}$
INCHES HIGH

SEE ALSO SCREEN NO. 32 ON THE NEXT PAGE, WHICH IS LARGER THAN
APPEARS, BEING 52 INCHES HIGH. WE HAVE PRETTY PATTERNS IN NEEDLE
POINT OR OTHER WORK, OR THE BUYERS MAY DO THAT PART OF THE WORK
THEMSELVES

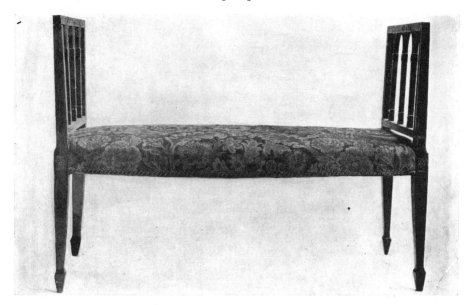

144   SHERATON WINDOW SEAT WITH CATHEDRAL
ARCH ENDS, 34 IN. LONG

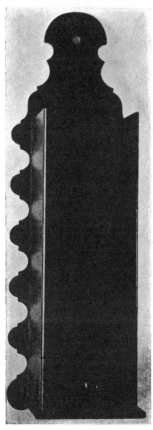

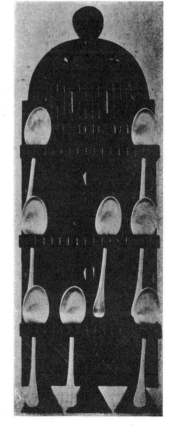

905   PIPE BOX, 22¾ IN.   32   903   SPOON RACK, 24¾ HIGH

161   14 X 20, 18 HIGH   164   18 HIGH

162   (IN FRONT) 72 X 18 X 14 LONG FORMS.
162B   36 X 18 X 14.
163   (BEHIND) 100 X 18 X 14

290   ALL MAPLE, 18 X 18 X 38

A ROOM SHOWING CARVED PHILADELPHIA LOWBOY, HIGHBOY, ARM AND SIDE PHILADELPHIA CARVED CHAIRS, WITH A CORNER OF A THREE CHAIR BACK SETTEE. THE BEST TYPE OF PIECRUST TABLE, A MIRROR OF VERY LARGE SIZE, AND A PORTION OF AN OXBOW CHEST OF DRAWERS

174   DUTCH, WALNUT, 20 X 14 X 15½ HIGH SLIP SEAT.
RUSHED OR UPHOLSTERED
174B   SAME, WITH SHELL ON KNEE

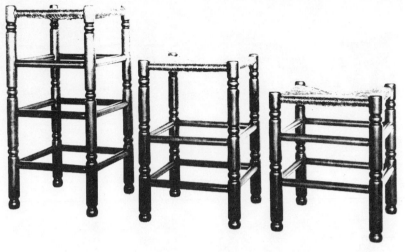

169 30 HIGH   168 22 HIGH   167 18 HIGH

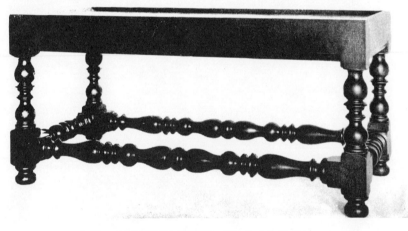

171 JACOBEAN STOOL, 30 X 14 X 14
SUPPLIED WITH LOOSE OR ATTACHED CUSHION ON ORDER

173 PINE TRESTLE STOOL, 18 X 14 X 65

165   JOINT, 15 HIGH, TOP, 12 X 20   166   RUSH, 15 HIGH, 15 SQUARE

102   $9\frac{1}{2}$ HIGH   101   8 HIGH   127 $9\frac{1}{2}$ HIGH

155   8 HIGH   107   8 HIGH   110   8 HIGH

153   8 HIGH   292 $4\frac{1}{2}$ HIGH   157 $9\frac{1}{2}$ HIGH

A ROOM OF THE EARLIEST TIME

179B   ALL CARVED, CHIPPENDALE STOOL
179   CARVED FEET ONLY

945   PINE, 37¾ X 19 X 80½ HIGH   944   PINE, 31¼ X 17 X 72¾ HIGH
945B   WITHOUT DOOR

The shelves of 945 and 945B have scrolled edges. There is a shelf below in this and in 944. They are the handsomest types ever discovered of pine corner cupboards, except the shell top, 925, shown elsewhere. They are beautifully made and are offered at very low prices, so that no one need buy modernistic horrors. Note the Queen Anne arches and scrolls. Mellow amber, or will be painted on order.

925 CARVED, PINE, 94 TO 99 HIGH, 48 WIDE
ADAPTED FOR SIDE OR CORNER

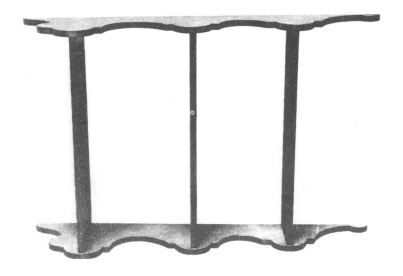

906 PINE, 19 WIDE, 30 HIGH

907 PINE, 36 WIDE, 43 HIGH

CUPBOARD PAGE 28
DOOR MAY BE OMITTED

927 PINE, $72\frac{1}{2}$ x 37 x 18
928 SAME, $72\frac{1}{2}$ x 49 x 18

40 HAT RACK, DIAM. $20\frac{3}{4}$

14 MAH. TRAY. 9 x $7\frac{3}{4}$ HIGH

926 PINE, 39 HIGH   923 PINE, 73 HIGH, 37 WIDE

The pine hanging corner cupboard above is the most attractive pattern that has come to our attention. It has butterfly hinges, the door end of which is mortised and bolted in the Pennsylvania fashion. The door is formed of one piece with cross sections fitted in to fill the mold. There is a little rim on the shelf below. I have been allowed to copy this by a dear friend.

923, the scrolled pewter cupboard on the right, is very popular as it fits in almost anywhere. There is a shelf behind the cupboard door.

942   PINE DRESSER, 75 HIGH, 50 WIDE, 18½ DEEP

Dressers are indicated to supply the place of sideboards in the maple period. Here let us say once for all that there is no pine period or maple period apart from each other. In the maple period the broad surfaces were usually in pine.

The dresser is convenient with its broad shelf and has plenty of storage room, and display room also for old china or pewter. 947, not shown, is built on substantially the same lines except that it is six feet wide, has devil tail hinges and the shelves are cut out to hang the pewter, in the Pennsylvania fashion.

922   OAK DRESSER, WELSH, 75½ x 54¼ x 18

All dressers are Welsh dressers in the loose jargon of the commercial furniture trade. The original of the piece above was imported by Wallace Nutting from Wales. Every part is in oak. The arched panels, lined, render the construction with its numerous drawers and paneled back more costly than the pine cupboards. The scrolled H hinges here and all the iron hardware examples are made by us, and invariably attached with hand made nails since their period is before the days of screws. The usual attachment by modern round headed screws is a ridiculous trimming which ruins the effect. In fact the almost uniform neglect of the proper hardware on colonial houses and furniture loses the sought for impression. We are specialists in that particular.

910   SUDBURY CUPBOARD, OAK 22½ X 54 X 55

THE FINEST AND EARLIEST AMERICAN CUPBOARD,
INLAY WALNUT AND MAPLE

This cupboard is perhaps the earliest style surviving in America. It is remarkable in being carved on the ends, the only American cupboard, possibly,
so made. The shelves are pine, moldings walnut, inlay, very thick, is maple
and walnut.

911   OAK, SUNFLOWER CUPBOARD, 21 X 48 X 57½

These cupboards are indicated for the furnishing of a dining room or den in the earliest American style. The originals have all been found in the East, and mostly in and near Hartford. They correspond to the " sunflower " or aster and tulip chest of the same origin. The originals are the most sought for of American antiques. Only those skilled in the lore of the subject fully appreciate such examples. It is for this reason that the discerning are buying these copies made in the same manner as the original with fat, bold turnings. The applied moldings are maroon. The channel molds and applied ornaments are black.

703B   TAMBOUR DESK. 703   WITHOUT TOP, 703C   INLAID

729   MAHOGANY DESK, 39½ HIGH, FRAME 36 X 19

AN OFFICE, WITH GREAT PEACOCK AND FLORAL RUG
BY MARIET G. NUTTING

731   CURLY OR PLAIN SECRETARY, 80 X 39½ X 20
730   SAME, LOWER PART ONLY, PLAIN OR CURLY

705   DESK ON CARVED FRAME, MAHOGANY
METROPOLITAN MUSEUM
706   DUTCH FOOT, NOT CARVED

42   43   44   45   46   47   48   49   50   51   52   53
      44B   48B

The finials above, another row of which is shown on page 95, are a part of the models in our possession. They cover all the periods, together with the drops. Some are very richly carved. The carved flutings on 50 and 51 do not show in the pictures. They extend around the urn. Any finial will be carved to order. Most of the above are in mahogany.

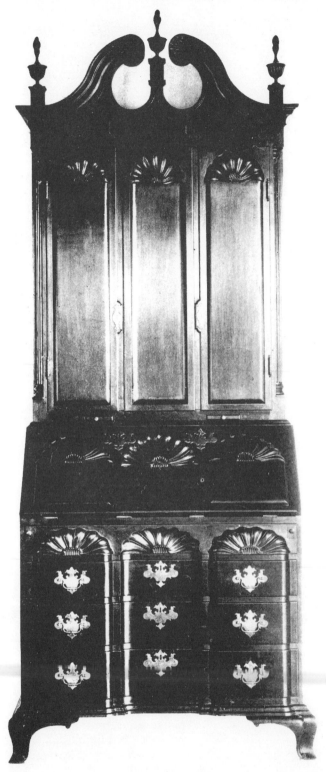

733   GODDARD SCHOOL, 104 x 39½ x 24

734   MAHOGANY, 44 X 39½ X 24. SEE OPPOSITE PAGE

AN OFFICE, WITH GREAT HOOKED RUG BY MRS. NUTTING

727 CURLY MAPLE, 40 X 26 X 18   700 OAK OR MAPLE, 33 X 25 X 19

DESK 727 HAS DARK LEGS AND FINIAL. DOOR CARVED FROM SOLID

701 SOLID MAPLE, 38½ HIGH, 41 LONG

710 WASHINGTON WRITING TABLE, SOLID MAHOGANY.
SHERATON TYPE. 71 LONG

627 LAZY SUSAN, MAHOGANY,
627B SAME, CARVED KNEE, CLAW FOOT

943 PINE, 21 X 15 X 64 HIGH
WILL BE MADE THINNER

740B   OX BOW, MAHOGANY SECRETARY   60   GODDARD TYPE
739   WITHOUT TOP. 740   BRACKET FOOT

SECRETARY IS 42 X 22¾ X 82½. OX BOW DRAWERS CUT FROM SINGLE PLANKS.
A MASSIVE BEAUTIFUL PIECE, WITH VERY HEAVY BALL FEET
THE CLOCK IS 94½ INCHES HIGH, OF HEAVY MAHOGANY, THE GODDARD
BLOCK AND SHELL PATTERN, CARVED FINIALS AND QUARTER COLUMNS
FOR ADAPTED DESKS SEE PAGE 140

991   MAPLE HIGHBOY, 77 HIGH, 34 WIDE
ALL MAPLE, MAHOGANY OR WALNUT, HAND DOVETAILED

989   MAHOGANY, $85\frac{1}{2}$ x $39\frac{1}{2}$ x 20

992   SAVERY SCHOOL, MAHOGANY HIGHBOY, 97 X 47 X 22$\frac{1}{2}$

988　RICHEST HIGHBOY, TO ORDER ONLY. METROPOLITAN
MUSEUM SPECIMEN

999　WALNUT HIGHBOY　　　　999B　SAME VENEERED
699　WALNUT LOWBOY TO MATCH　　699B　SAME VENEERED

1000   GODDARD TYPE, BLOCK AND SHELL CHEST ON CHEST.
DELICATELY CARVED URNS. 81 HIGH X $41\frac{3}{4}$ WIDE X $21\frac{3}{4}$ DEEP

934   SHERATON, INLAID CHEST OF DRAWERS, TURNED, REEDED AND CARVED
LEGS VENEERED WITH PLUMED GRAIN SATINWOOD. CURVED FRONT

This piece represents development at the close of the eighteenth century when a large feature was made of delicate lines and selected veneers.

The original is in the furnishings of Mr. Nutting's home. He had the piece from his nurse.

We show on page 55 an oxbow chest of drawers which is a reversed serpentine. We will make to order the usual serpentine chest of drawers if desired with bracket or ball feet. The earliest fine type has a chamfered corner.

979   GODDARD STYLE, BLOCK FRONT CHEST OF DRAWERS,
SCROLLED FOOT

918   BLOCK FRONT, MAHOGANY, 30 HIGH, TOP 35 X 20

916   MAPLE, PLAIN OR CURLY, 37 HIGH, TOP 38 X 19

941   MAHOGANY, QUARTER COLUMN, 37 X 38 X 19

952 KNEE HOLE, FOUR SHELL, GODDARD "BUREAU TABLE," SAN
DOMINGO MAHOGANY, 37 X 20 X 34 HIGH. SCROLLED FOOT

180 CHIPPENDALE STOOL, MAHOGANY, MOLDED STRAIGHT LEG,
STRETCHERS, SLIP SEAT

A ROOM IN QUEEN ANNE TYPE. RUG BY MRS. NUTTING

919   OX BOW, HEAVY MAHOGANY, 38 LONG X 20 X 37 HIGH
919B   BRACKET FOOT

915   PINE, $39\frac{1}{2}$ X 38 X 19

175   SIGN, LETTERED, 36 X 24   920   CHEST-ON-FRAME, 34 X 28 X $19\frac{1}{2}$

913   ALL PINE CHEST OF DRAWERS, SCROLLED BOARD FEET. SIMPLE TYPE
OPTION OF HALF ROUND MOLD AROUND DRAWERS
10% MORE. $39\frac{1}{2}$ X 38 X 19

WOODEN UTENSILS IN CURLY MAPLE, EXCEPT 19, WHICH IS MAHOGANY
25B   GOBLET; 19   WAFER URN; 10   SHOT WELL; 31   CANDLESTICKS;
25 AND 29   CUP AND SAUCER

937   OAK, 39 WIDE, 42 HIGH

936   PANELED, QUARTERED OAK, 40 WIDE, 42 HIGH
958   SAME WITH APPLIED SPINDLE DECORATION

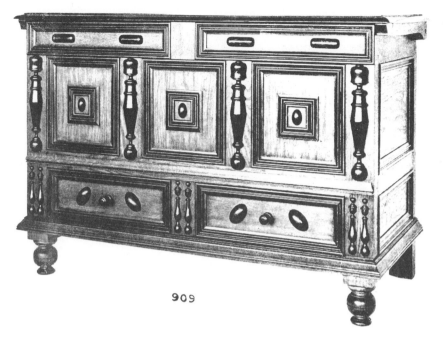

909

909   OAK, ONE DRAWER CHEST, 21 X $47\frac{3}{4}$ X $34\frac{1}{2}$
ORNAMENTS IN BLACK

933

933   OAK, NORMAN TOOTH, 20 X $33\frac{1}{2}$ X 40

900   BIBLE BOX, 9 X 17 X 25, OAK

THESE BOXES ARE MINIATURE CHESTS AND ARE NOT ONLY CONVENIENT AND
PORTABLE, BUT DECORATIVE IN THE HIGHEST DEGREE. THE LID
AND BASE ARE PINE

The miniature chests are now used for silver chests and will be fitted with
trays and the best locks for that purpose, to order.
See the other pattern on the next page

938   PENNSYLVANIA PANELED, PAINTED, TWO DRAWER CHEST.
BRILLIANT COLORING. PERIOD 1785

A REMARKABLY ATTRACTIVE EXAMPLE. $52\frac{1}{2}$ LONG, 30 HIGH, $24\frac{1}{2}$ DEEP
FITTED WITH OLD TYPE WROUGHT LOCK AND LONG HINGES.

931   OAK, SUNFLOWER CHEST, 48 LONG, 20 DEEP, 42 HIGH

THIS FINE TYPE, ALL ORIGINALS OF WHICH WERE MADE IN OR NEAR HART-
FORD PROBABLY IS A REMARKABLE EXAMPLE; MATCHES COURT CUPBOARD
ON PAGE 35. ORNAMENTS BLACK; ALSO CHANNEL MOLDS
THE APPLIED MOLDINGS ARE IN MAROON VERGING TO RED

901   OAK, 10 X 27 X 17, SPACE FOR INITIALS

935   OAK, HADLEY CHEST, SPACE FOR INITIALS, 48 WIDE, 46 HIGH

Chests of this type belong near the end of the 17th century. Tulip carving is the usual decoration. This example is far above the average artistically, because the carving on rails and stiles runs as a continuous scroll.

452   CARVED AND INLAID, SCROLLED ARM, SHERATON,
MARTHA WASHINGTON. THIS CHAIR IS THE MOST
DAINTY DEVELOPMENT OF ITS PERIOD

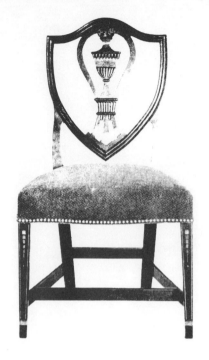

332   CONN. SENATE CHAIR. MAH.
432   ARM CHAIR TO MATCH

342   MAHOGANY CARVED
342B CARVING OMITTED

335   SHERATON, CARVED, MAH.
435   ARM CHAIR TO MATCH

435   LIGHT MARTHA WASH'N.
      SEE ALSO 452

338 WHEAT EAR HEPPLEWHITE   438 WHEAT EAR, MOLDED ARM
SHAPED SEAT. TAPER LEGS   ARM DOVETAILED TO SEAT

372 SIDE. 472 ARM. DAINTY ADAM TYPES

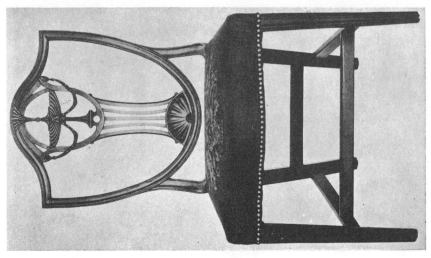

337 GODDARD TYPE. EXQUISITE BACK KNOWN AS THE EGYPTIAN WING TYPE

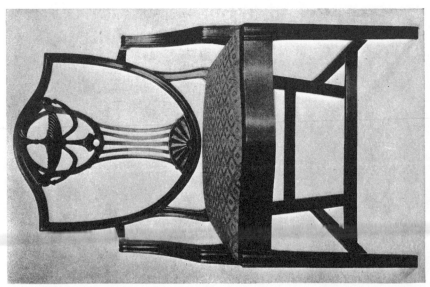

437 GODDARD TYPE. DAINTEST HEPPLEWHITE COMPARES FAVORABLY WITH 456, R. I. TYPE

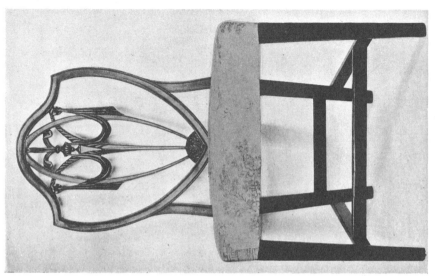

371 HEPPLEWHITE, FEATHERS AND DRAPERY
471 ARM CHAIR. ALWAYS MAHOGANY

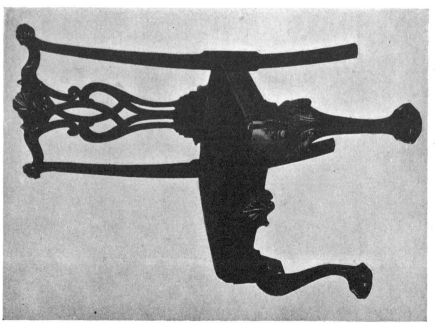

343 A RICH CHIPPENDALE CHAIR WITH A FULLY
CARVED BACK, ENGRAILED. ORNAMENTED SEAT RAIL

434   PHILADELPHIA CHIPPENDALE
FULLY CARVED. MAHOGANY,
$18\frac{1}{4}$ x $23\frac{3}{4}$ x 39 HIGH

334   PHILADELPHIA CHIPPENDALE,
FULLY CARVED. MAHOGANY,
17 x $21\frac{1}{2}$ x 39 HIGH

363   OPTION, 363B   CARVED

473   LEATHER OR FABRIC

359 CARVED, SIDE
459 ARM CHAIR SAME STYLE

496B CHIP. CORNER, $33\frac{1}{2}$ X 28, OR
496 KNEE CARVING OMITTED

359B CARVED. FOUR LADDER
459B ARM. ALWAYS MAHOGANY

362 THREE SLATS ONLY. UNCARVED
462 ARM, THREE BACK, MAHOGANY

466   MAHOGANY, CARVED KNEE, BALL FOOT, CHIPPENDALE WING CHAIR
THE RICHEST TYPE. CUSHION WITH DOWN. BUILT LIKE A SHIP

This wing chair is sometimes found without stretchers, and if so made the discount of 10% will be allowed. We use in these chairs down at $3 a pound mingled with feathers for the cushion, and for the upholstery as all our upholstery superfine white curled hair throughout.

The wing chair while exceedingly popular at the present time is scarcely more comfortable than the pine wing chair if supplied with a deep cushion, as shown on page 91, for a simple house or for a den.

627 MAHOGANY, 46 HIGH
SCREEN, 18½ x 15½

465 WALNUT, FINE, 48 x 31½ x 25

356 MAHOGANY, 39 x 23½ x 17

456 MAHOGANY, 39 x 25 x 18¼

398   WALNUT, 40½ x 19¾ x 15½   498   WALNUT, 40½ x 21½ x 17½

HANDSOMER AND IN BETTER STYLE THAN ANY OTHER QUEEN ANNE MODEL

458   MAHOGANY, 37½ x 23 x 18¾   358   MAHOGANY, 37½ x 21½ x 18½

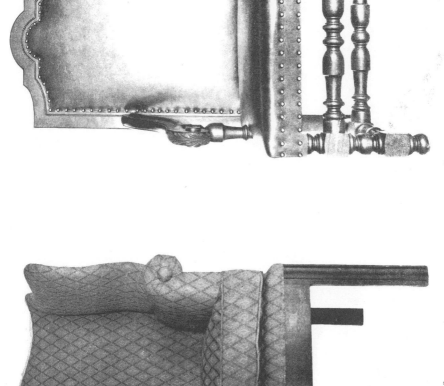

481   LEATHER EASY ELBOW CHAIR, LOW SEAT

468   CHIPPENDALE WING. 468B   WITH STRETCHERS

399 RAMPED BACK, SIDE
499 RAMPED BACK, ARM

399B WALNUT, SCROLLED
499B ARM, OPTION, BALL FEET

338B FLUTED REED BACK
438B ARM. MAHOGANY

499C QUEEN ANNE, WALNUT
399C SIDE CHAIR TO MATCH

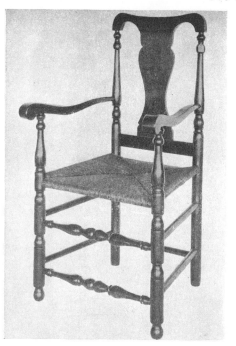

461   COUNTRY DUTCH TYPE, ARM
41 x 22$\frac{1}{2}$ x 17$\frac{1}{2}$

361   DUTCH, 41 x 19$\frac{1}{2}$ x 15
SIMPLE, EFFECTIVE, INEXPENSIVE

204   CHILD'S THREE BACK
SEAT 9 HIGH, TOTAL HEIGHT 30

211   CHILD'S COMB BACK
A PERFECT MINIATURE

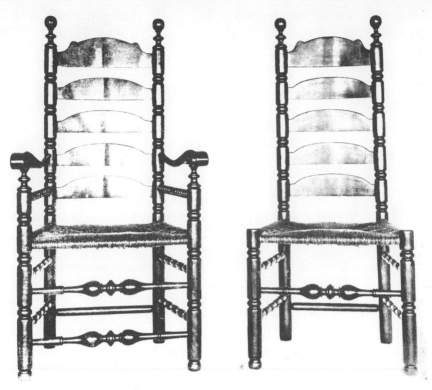

490 MAPLE, 50 HIGH   390 MAPLE, 50 HIGH

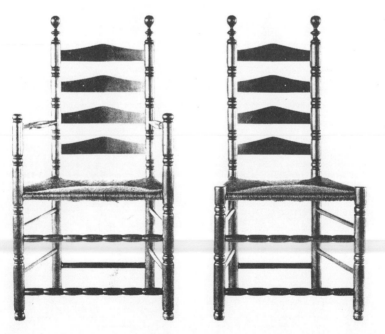

492 FOUR BACK, $44\frac{1}{2}$ x $23\frac{1}{2}$ 392 FOUR BACK, SIDE, $44\frac{1}{2}$ HIGH

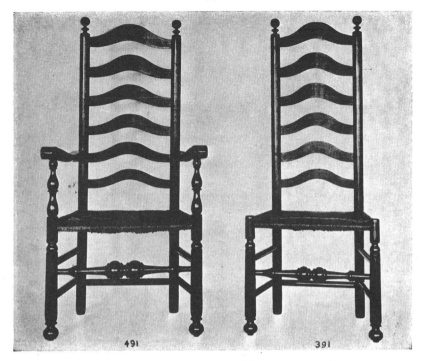

491 MAPLE, 53 HIGH 391 MAPLE, 53 HIGH
A DELAWARE VALLEY SIX BACK. PERFECT FOR HALL

414 LIKE 415 WITHOUT UPPER BACK 413 LOW BACK, ARM, 31 X 25 X 18

375   FIDDLE BACK. OR CARVED SADDLE
375B SAME, TURNED FOOT. MAPLE
475   FIDDLE BACK, SPANISH, ARM

374   LIGHT THREE BACK, MAPLE
THE SIMPLEST RUSH SEAT TYPE
475B FIDDLE BACK, TURNED FOOT

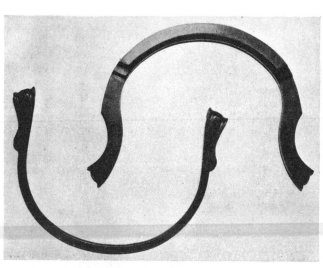

ABOVE, ARM RAIL OF 415 AND 420
BELOW 407 AND 408

480   MAPLE, 50 HIGH   380   MAPLE, 50 HIGH

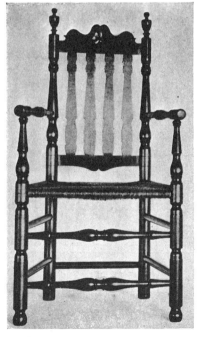

465B   WILD ROSE, 45 HIGH   365   WILD ROSE, 45 HIGH

411   BREWSTER, MAPLE, $46\frac{1}{2}$ HIGH   360   CROMWELLIAN, 39 HIGH

364   CARVER SIDE, 45 HIGH   464   CARVER ARM, MAPLE, 47 HIGH

493 PILGRIM, MAPLE, 47 X 24¾   393 PILGRIM SIDE, 43 HIGH
THE MOST MASSIVE AND MOST COMFORTABLE OF ALL EARLY CHAIRS

394 WALNUT SIDE, 46 HIGH   494 WALNUT ARM, 22 WIDE

476   FLEMISH, MAPLE
CARVED PANEL ADDITIONAL

355   HIGH DESK, 22 INCH SEAT
TOTAL HEIGHT 45 INCHES

310   AN EXCELLENT CHAIR
37 INCHES HIGH. REGULAR SEAT

349   SLIPPER CHAIR. 15 IN HIGH
FULL SIZE SEAT

493B MAPLE, PILGRIM, 47 HIGH
A LIGHTER CHAIR THAN 493

407 LIGHT BACK, 44 HIGH
BENT ARM, KNUCKLE

402 LADY'S, 46 HIGH

333 44 HIGH

408   BENT ARM, WINDSOR BOW BACK. A PERFECT TYPE
LIGHT WEIGHT, SHAPED SEAT, CARVED ARM, VASE LEG

420 BOW BACK, 41 HIGH

301 39 HIGH

415 COMB BACK, 45 HIGH

326 41 HIGH

430   CORNER, MAPLE, $24\frac{1}{2}$ X $32\frac{1}{2}$ 22   CROSS BASE CANDLESTAND, $25\frac{1}{2}$ X 14

305 BENT RUNG. 304 STRAIGHT RUNG   404 BABY'S HIGH

401   ONE PIECE BOW AND ARM, BRACED. VERY LIGHT
A PERFECT LADY'S CHAIR. MEDIUM SIZE. DAINTY

412   49 HIGH

309   MATCHING 412

421   49 HIGH

422   47 HIGH

440   ARM, 48 HIGH, TABLE, 18 WIDE   329   SWIVEL, 40 X 18 X 16¾

A SEVENTEENTH CENTURY DINING ROOM

451   ARM IS 17 WIDE

24   COSTUMER, 67 HIGH

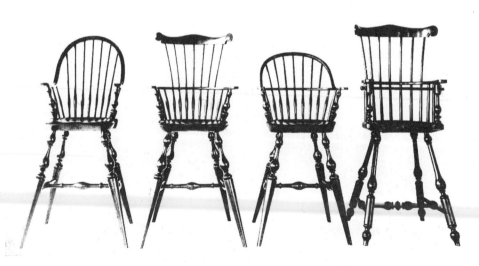

210   201   205   209

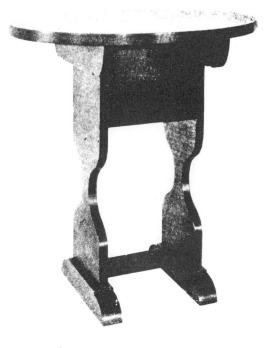

416   PINE, WING, 24 X 22 X 46¾
HIGH. BOX BELOW SEAT

654   PINE HUTCH TABLE
17¾ X 24½ HIGH

513   PINE SETTLE, 70 X 22 X 46¾ HIGH. SEAT HINGED
BOX BELOW. PANELS, SEAT, AND FRONT BASE IN SINGLE BOARDS

564   MAPLE LOVE SEAT, 18 X 47

THE MOST BEAUTIFUL KNOWN WINDSOR SETTEE
IN TWIN CHAIR FORM ROLLED BACK

589   AMERICAN MAPLE AND PINE WAINSCOT SETTLE. UNIQUE

WALLACE NUTTING COLLECTION, HARTFORD. $75\frac{3}{4}$ X $20\frac{1}{2}$ X $50\frac{3}{4}$

533   LOW BACK PENNSYLVANIA TEN LEGGER, 18 x 89

594   COMB BACK TEN LEGGER, 18 x 89

515   TRIPLE BOW BACK TEN LEGGER, 18 x 89

591   TRIPLE FIVE BACK, 50 HIGH, 63 LONG
DIGNITY, STYLE, BEAUTY, STRENGTH, FOR PUBLIC ROOMS

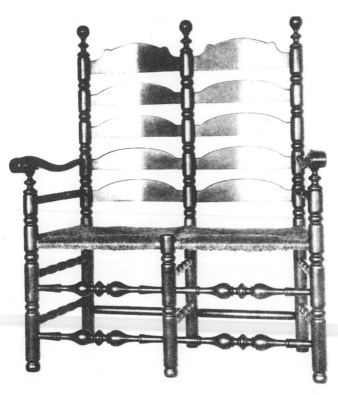

590   DOUBLE FIVE BACK, 50 HIGH, 44 LONG

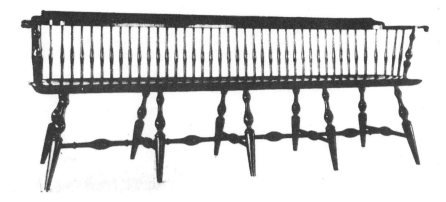

514   LOW BACK TEN LEGGER, 18 x 89

545   COMB BACK TEN LEGGER, 89 LONG

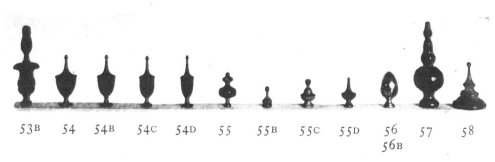

53B   54   54B   54C   54D   55   55B   55C   55D   56   57   58
                                                                  56B

FINIALS SUPPLEMENTING OTHERS SHOWN ON PAGE 39

539   SHERATON SOFA, MAHOGANY. POSTS INLAID AND REEDED. 82 x 24
WILL BE MADE 66 OR 72 INCHES LONG AT PROPORTIONATE COST
579   SHERATON THREE CHAIR SETTEE LIKE CHAIR 335
568B   CHIPPENDALE SOFA, 60 INCHES, LIKE WING CHAIR 468B

569   CHIP. THREE CHAIR, FRENCH SCROLL FOOT, MAHOGANY. LINEN FOLD
ENGRAILED FRAME. PROPERTY OF MR. NUTTING. MADE OF THREE CHAIRS
599   WALNUT SETTEE. LIKE CHAIR 399 (THREE BACK)

534   PHILADELPHIA CHIPPENDALE. FULLY CARVED LOVE SEAT. HEAVY
MAHOGANY, $48\frac{1}{2}$ X 39 HIGH
ROPE MOLDS, ROLLED EARS, CARVED ARMS AND ARM POSTS

534B   THREE CHAIR BACK PHILADELPHIA CHIPPENDALE SETTEE
RICHLY CARVED. 67 X $18\frac{1}{2}$ X $39\frac{1}{4}$. SLIP SEAT

525 CHIPPENDALE (SIX LEG, 62 LONG) FOUR LEG SOFA
OVER ALL DIMENSIONS, 48 LONG, 31 DEEP, 37 HIGH
538 THREE CHAIR BACK, STYLE OF CHAIR 438

559 FOUR LADDER BACK, THREE CHAIR SETTEE, MAHOGANY. ALL LEGS
AND MEMBERS MOLDED. THE PICTURE IS THAT FURNISHED
556 THREE CHAIR BACK, STYLE OF CHAIR 456

AN ALL CURLY BED ROOM. RUG, $6\frac{1}{2}$ X $8\frac{1}{2}$ FEET, BY MRS. NUTTING

615   TRESTLE, ALL MAPLE, 30 X 50, OR 30 X 60
THESE TABLES ARE USED IN PAIRS, TANDEM OR IN SPAN

THIS BRAND MUST APPEAR ON ALL MY FURNITURE

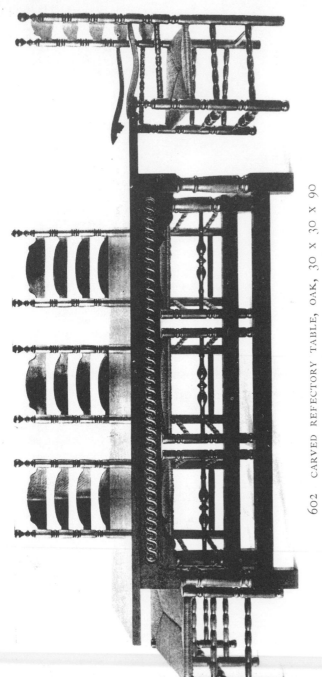

602   CARVED REFECTORY TABLE, OAK, 30 × 30 × 90

618   PENSHURST TRESTLE, OAK TOP, 30 × $40\frac{1}{2}$ × 108, OR 180 LONG × 42 WIDE

612B EARLIEST AMERICAN TRESTLE. MAPLE FRAME, PINE TOP. 132 X 30 X 30

638 LIBRARY, REFECTORY OR DIRECTORS' TABLE. WALNUT OR MAPLE OR MAPLE PINE TOP. NEVER MAHOGANY. DRAWERS OMITTED, 5% LESS. 120 X 39½

601   BRACKET REFECTORY, OAK, 30 X 30 X 90
607   SIX LEG, TEN FEET LONG. 607B   CARVED ON BOTH SIDES
607C SAME, 36 X 156, SIX LEGS, CARVED ON BOTH SIDES. SEE 602

610

610   OAK TOP, 30 X 36 X 72   611   30 X 30 X 108
        612 36 X 120   BASES IN MAPLE

617   PINE VASE TRESTLE, A SWEDISH TYPE, 30 X 37 X 86

603   SOLID MAPLE, 29¾ HIGH, TOP 44 X 52
(WIDE OVERHANG ALL AROUND)

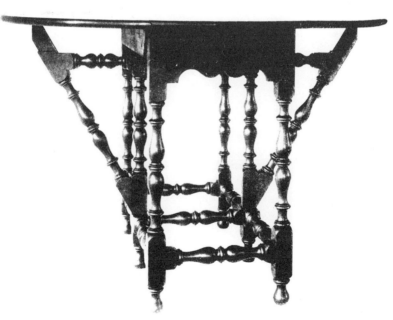

619   SOLID MAPLE, 28 HIGH, TOP 36½ X 41
THE MOST BEAUTIFUL OF TABLES — A CRANE BRACKET

636 SUPREME GATE LEG, 30 X 72 X 78, MAPLE OR WALNUT
THE PROPER TABLE FOR A GREAT DINING OR DIRECTORS' ROOM

621 MAPLE, LIGHT FOUR GATE, 30 X 48 X 59
622 SAME, HEAVIER TURNING, 30 X 60 X 70
631 SAME AS 622, BUT WITH ONLY TWO GATES

622B   SPANISH FOOT, TWELVE LEG, FOUR GATE, WALNUT OR MAPLE. 60 X 70

697   QUEEN ANNE CARD TABLE. WALNUT, SLIGHTLY CARVED. 33 X 32 X 28

620 SPANISH FOOT GATE LEG, 48 X 59. MAPLE, WALNUT TO ORDER
632 SAME, PLAIN FOOT, 48 X 59. USUALLY MAPLE, WALNUT OPTIONAL

698B WALNUT, QUEEN ANNE SERVING TABLE, 66 LONG

660   MAPLE, PINE TOP, 24 x 36 x $26\frac{3}{4}$
THE OLDEST TYPE OF TAVERN TABLE

626   MAPLE, DRESSING, 28 HIGH, TOP $31\frac{1}{2}$ x $21\frac{1}{4}$
MADE ALSO IN WALNUT. TRUMPET TURNED

634　CHIPPENDALE CARD TABLE, BALL AND CLAW, CARVED KNEE,
CARVED SCROLLED FRAME

681　THREE PART, MAHOGANY, 47 WIDE, BY 121. TWO LEAVES
681B PLAIN TOP. 681C　TWO PART, PLAIN, 47 X 74
THESE PHYFE TABLES WILL BE MADE IN FOUR PARTS AT PROPORTIONATE
PRICES. HEAVY BRASS "ANIMAL" FEET. THE DOUBLE TABLE IS PROVIDED
WITH ONE, THE TRIPLE TABLE WITH TWO EXTRA LEAVES, AND SO ON.
BRASS CLIPS AND BUTTONS CONNECT THE PARTS

637 MAPLE, 30 X 30 X 50, ROOM FOR KNEES

659 MAHOGANY, FLUTED LEGS, 48 SQUARE

3 FRAME. 4 PEPPER. I FRAME. 5 SHAKER. 2 FRAME

655   MAPLE, 26¼ HIGH, TOP 24½ X 31

613   MAPLE, 27½ HIGH, PINE TOP 36 X 25½

648 ROUND CHIPPENDALE, DIAMETER 48. ALSO OFFERED WITH DUTCH
OR PAD FOOT 10% LESS. MAHOGANY WITH OPTION OF MAPLE. END SCROLL

604 COUNTRY DUTCH, TAVERN, PORRINGER CORNER. 36 X 23 X 28$\frac{3}{4}$ HIGH

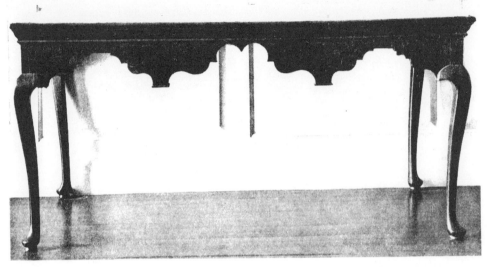

667   WALNUT, DUTCH SERVING TABLE. UNIQUE PATTERN. 72 LONG

698   WALNUT CARVED SIDEBOARD, $32\frac{1}{2}$ HIGH, TOP 22 X 42

We advise the use of a sideboard table in walnut or mahogany for the Queen Anne and Chippendale periods. The sideboard comes in the Hepplewhite and Sheraton time, and is a considerable declension in style; nevertheless we make sideboards of various sizes.

683B SIDEBOARD, VENEERED WITH SATINWOOD, BANDED WITH BLACK AND WHITE LINES, AND EDGED WITH A BAND OF MAHOGANY VENEER ON MAHOGANY

650 CHIPPENDALE HALL OR SIDEBOARD. METROPOLITAN MUSEUM
OFFERED ALSO WITHOUT CARVING ON THE FRAME, OR IN PART

683 PLAIN MAHOGANY. DOUBLE SCROLL. $70\frac{1}{4}$ X 29 X $38\frac{3}{4}$. 683B SAME SIZE

695   MAHOGANY, 33 DIAMETER
SNAKE FOOT, DISHED TOP

694   WALNUT, 33 DIAMETER. DISH TOP
ALSO PLAIN. MADE ALSO SMALLER

ALL OUR TIP TABLES WITH A SHAFT OR STANDARD HAVE THE SPREADING
LEGS VERY PERFECTLY DOVETAILED INTO THE POSTS, AND ARE SUPPORTED
IN ADDITION IN THE OLD FASHION BY A BRACING IRON UNDERNEATH

680   MAHOGANY, THREE, FOUR, OR FIVE PART, 48 WIDE, LENGTH FROM
119 TO 209 INCHES. MADE WITH OR WITHOUT CARVED KNEE
680B   MADE WITH DUTCH (PAD) FOOT

670   HEPPLEWHITE THREE PART TABLE, LEGS INLAID. EXTENDED 48 x 96

668   SHERATON, MAHOGANY CARD, INLAID AND VENEERED. 33 x 32 x 28

689   MAHOGANY LOWBOY MATCHING HIGHBOY 989   36 x $20\frac{1}{2}$ x $29\frac{1}{2}$
LOCKED DRAWERS. SHELL DEEPLY CUT WITH CURVE. EXCELLENT

699   SOLID WALNUT LOWBOY, TO ACCOMPANY 999,
PAGE 49, BUT MADE SINGLE ARCH MOLD

691   MAPLE LOWBOY, $29\frac{1}{2}$ x 39 x $20\frac{1}{2}$

692   SAVERY SCHOOL, $29\frac{1}{2}$ x 34 x 20

THE QUARTER COLUMNS, THE INCISED AND APPLIED CARVING COVERING
THE FULL LENGTH OF THE SKIRT, THE RICH KNEE AND FOOT AND CLOVER
LEAF CORNER DECORATE THIS RICH PHILADELPHIA STYLE LOWBOY.
THE PIECE MATCHES THE HIGHBOY 992, ALSO SHOWN

693B   RICH EXAMPLE OF THE PIECRUST. FOOT IN ONE PIECE ABOUT FOUR
INCHES WIDE. HEAVY TOP. 693 OMITS CARVING
EXCEPT ON FOOT. 33 X 27½ HIGH

628   MAHOGANY PEMBROKE,
36 X 36 X 28¼

629   HEPPLEWHITE PEMBROKE.
33 X 36

616 28 HIGH, TOP 25 X 35
A TUCKAWAY GATE LEG. STYLISH

653 24 HIGH, 21 DIAMETER
ALL LEGS RAKED. PINE TOP

18 25 X 12

614 27 HIGH, PINE TOP 19 X 30

623   25 HIGH, TOP 29 X 36   624   26½ HIGH, TOP 30 X 40

ALL BUTTERFLY TABLES ARE ALL SOLID MAPLE

625   26½ HIGH, TOP 26 X 29½   21   MAPLE, 36 HIGH

23　BOOK OR MUSIC REST, 37 HIGH　647　SNAKE FOOT, TOP 18 DIAMETER

608　OCTAGON, SPLINE. 18 X 18 X 29　643　MAHOGANY 14$\frac{1}{4}$ X 14$\frac{1}{4}$ X 27$\frac{1}{4}$

MAPLE, MAH., OR MAPLE WITH MAH. LEG　CORNER SPLINED. DOVETAILED

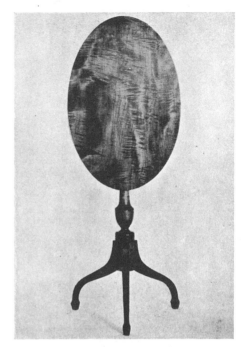

664   MAHOG. FULLY CARVED   644   HEPPLEWHITE TRIPOD. 16 X 24. MAPLE
18 X 27¾ HIGH   SAME, MAHOG. INLAID. MAPLE 33% LESS

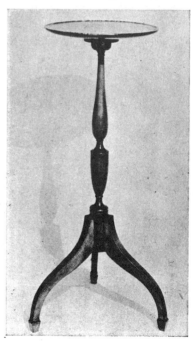

696   CURLY, 18 DIAMETER, 24½ HIGH   606   CURLY TOP, 34½ X 13½
696B SAME, RAISED RIM TOP   MOST GRACEFUL. OPTION MAHOGANY

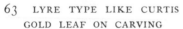

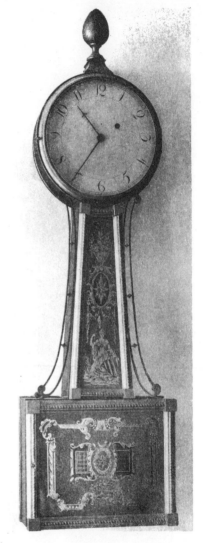

63   LYRE TYPE LIKE CURTIS   61   BANJO, DISHED DIAL. 33 HIGH
GOLD LEAF ON CARVING   CHOICE OF GLASSES. BRACKET ADDED

FOR ANOTHER CLOCK SEE PAGE 44

A GREAT ROOM WITH 636, 292, 655, 900, 907 AND 493

65   RICHEST GODDARD TYPE. 94 HIGH   71   BLOCK FRONT, MAHOGANY

68B   PHILADELPHIA TYPE. $93\frac{1}{2}$ HIGH   59B   WILLARD TYPE, INLAID, 94 HIGH

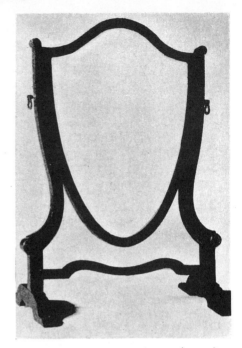

WE PRESENT TWO ATTRACTIVE SHAVING OR DRESSING GLASSES. 770 (LEFT)
IN CURLY MAPLE, MAHOGANY OR WALNUT. 19 X 13½ OVER ALL.
771 (RIGHT) 18 INCHES HIGH, IN MAHOGANY
WITH DECORATIVE ROSETTES

18 X 28   18 HIGH   25 X 14

769   HEPPLEWHITE FILIGREE TOP, INLAID MAHOGANY AND GOLD GLASS.
THE WHEAT EARS, FLOWERS, URN, ROSETTES AND SWAG ARE ALL CARVED
BASSWOOD, GILDED. BUTTERFLY INLAYS. $21\frac{1}{2}$ X 64 OUTSIDE
THIS GLASS IS THE HIGHEST TYPE IN ITS CLASS
ALL OUR MIRRORS OF EVERY SIZE AND PRICE ARE FILLED WITH
HEAVY PLATE GLASS
765   (RIGHT) CHIPPENDALE, MAHOGANY, INLAID, WITH CARVED GOLD
EAGLE AND SMALL ROSETTES. $52\frac{1}{2}$ X 24 OUTSIDE

The glass 757, on another page is one of the finest and largest ever reproduced. The original is in the Wallace Nutting collection
at the Atheneum, Hartford.

774   WALNUT, 24¾ X 13½,
GLASS 16¾ X 10¼

772   SAME WITHOUT TOP SCROLL

760   CURLY, GLASS, 17¼ X 34¾
ALSO IN MAHOGANY   760

761   MAPLE, GOLD FEATHER,
34½ X 17, GLASS, 11½ X 20¾

763   WALNUT AND GOLD, 32 X 13¼
GLASS, 10¼ X 16½

751   WALNUT, 22½ X 42
GLASS, 14½ X 23¼

750   OAK, 24½ X 36
GLASS, 15½ X 23½

755   WALNUT, 16 X 42
LOWER GLASS, 13¼ X 23¼

754   MAPLE, 19 X 34
GLASS, 13½ X 21½

757 MAHOGANY AND GOLD, 69 HIGH, 34 WIDE
GLASS, 35 X 22. ALL CARVED

773 WALNUT LOVE BIRD GLASS, GOLD ORNAMENTS. 15 X 38. QUEEN ANNE

764 MAHOGANY, WITH GOLD INTAGLIO BIRD LATE QUEEN ANNE TYPE. 41½ LONG

753   THREE PART MANTEL GLASS. THREE LARGE UPPER GLASSES ARE ELE-
GANTLY PAINTED BY THE BEST MODERN MASTER OF THE ART.
ALL OTHER PARTS GOLD LEAF. SIZE 60 X 29, OVER ALL

PICTURES

The Wallace Nutting pictures have maintained and still maintain an un-
questioned lead among such subjects. Their range is very broad, including
so called colonial subjects, being interiors and exteriors of old houses,
autumnal scenes, apple blossoms, birches, streams, gardens, and cottages
throughout America, the British Isles and western Europe. They include
many architectural themes, admirable for decoration. These latter will be
supplied in black and white, or in color.

All pictures are sold through the trade and will not be sold direct except
at great distances from any representative. Our furniture on the contrary is
sold direct. A catalogue of the pictures is out of the question.

Sizes: 8 x 10, mounted 13 x 16, $3, or $5 framed. 11 x 14, mounted 16 x
20, $6, or $9.50 framed. 16 x 20, mounted 26 x 30, $11, or $16.50 framed.
5 x 7, mounted 10 x 12, $1.50, or $2.75 framed.

There are twelve other sizes larger or smaller, from the 20 x 40 at $24, to
the $3\frac{1}{4}$ x 4, mounted 7 x 9, at $1 framed, in a box.

The prices above are for very carefully hand colored work. We do not
sell blossom and garden pictures in black and white, but architectural things
will be sold at half the above prices. Customers may order us to send goods
to their nearest dealer.

The superiority of these pictures to the usual cheap etching repeated in
public rooms *ad nauseam* is obvious. Particularly our great line of colonial
subjects has no counterpart in anything else offered.

As we are ourselves interior decorators, we can give other decorators
merely a courtesy commission of ten per cent. The discerning will quickly
understand that as a rule interior decorators fail to recommend as desirable
any furniture or pictures on which they cannot obtain a discount of at least a
third. We are glad to give decorators a courtesy commission on furniture, but
long experience has taught us that we cannot afford to sell less than our
public prices and that shops feeling they must, naturally, obtain a great
advance cannot successfully handle our furniture. This does not hold true
of pictures.

THOUSANDS OF INTERIORS AND EXTERIORS 8 X 10 OR 11 X 14 AND LARGER.
PLAIN OR COLORED. EUROPEAN ARCHITECTURAL THEMES

CALENDARS

CALENDARS OF ALL SIZES ARE SUPPLIED IN MANY PATTERNS BESIDES THOSE ABOVE.
THE PRICES RANGE ABOUT 20% HIGHER THAN THE PICTURES OF THE SAME SIZE.
THE PICTURES ARE PRESERVED AFTER THE CALENDAR YEAR EXPIRES

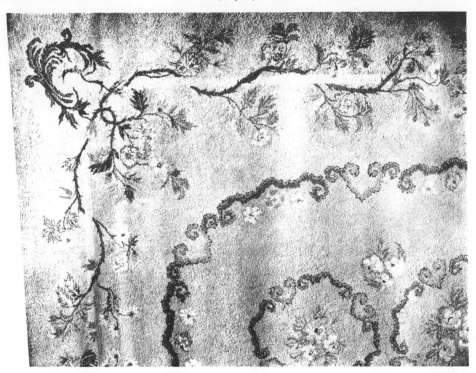

RUGS

On several pages, as 37, 41, 55, rugs have been shown with furniture. Above is shown one quarter of a rug with more detail.

No small rugs are made except to order, our thought being to supply what hitherto has not been available, namely, rugs with ancient motives, drawn in, in quaint and fine designs and of size sufficient for a room. Hence most of our rugs, which have been entirely created by Mrs. Wallace Nutting, are twelve by fourteen feet in size. They are made on single pieces of burlap specially made for us abroad in twelve foot wide rolls, to avoid all pieces.

The drawing in is with coarse yarns of wools specially prepared for this purpose. It was necessary to make metal rolls to sustain these large rugs in working. We use no stencils, but a photographic method developed by Mr. Nutting to secure faithful reproduction of the design supplied by Mrs. Nutting.

The designs are in grounds of olive, blue and other colors, and include bird and flower patterns.

The rugs are hooked with utmost care and the thirty-two colors, which we have dyed for us, are blended softly to produce the most harmonious effects.

We also make a rug about six and a half by eight and a half of a bluebell pattern, and can of course make intermediate sizes.

These rugs are better for our furniture than anything else, and though of course these sizes are not cheap they compare favorably with oriental rugs of good quality.

We desire to avoid repetition and hence make no two rugs just alike.

We do not wish to send these rugs about the country. Our friends find it worth while to come to us. At present we have four of the largest size in stock.

BOOKS

Above is shown a few of the books by Wallace Nutting. The " Furniture Treasury " is the last and most important work he has issued. It consists of five thousand pictures, fifteen hundred thirty-six large octavo pages in two volumes. The work represents the researches and accumulation of twenty years, and was issued at an expense of sixty-five thousand dollars, and is naturally the fullest work on the subject. The binding is the best, being heavily reënforced, and the paper and the brown tone printing are the highest quality. This work on a commercial basis would naturally sell at $40. The popular price of $25 for the set has been made; $26, library edition, uncut, gilt top; $40, three quarter leather with a full page hand colored antique interior, signed, in each volume. This is the edition shown on the right.

Of the nine volumes in the States Beautiful series, each with three hundred four pages, and three hundred four pictures, the only ones not out of print are England and New York. The Clock Book is also out of print, but very much more material on clocks is contained in the volumes of the " Furniture Treasury."

The author has in mind the publication of further books of the States Beautiful series and he has the material in part for California, Florida and other states. The exigencies of life, however, render it inadvisable for him to make a proposed date of publication.

" Photographic Art Secrets " is still available, a book richly illustrated with a variety of subjects in many parts of the world, and descriptive of the methods of art photography. Price $3.

A prospectus of " Furniture Treasury " will be sent on request. It is a necessity and a delight to all interested in the styles of American furniture.

LECTURES

The Wallace Nutting lantern slides cover about three thousand subjects. Six lectures cover the entire period of American Homes and Furnishings. There are also lectures on the various states, including England and Ireland and the continent, showing themes of general interest, and extending to twenty-four subjects including some of the purely literary character without pictures. These lectures are popular for all sorts of organizations, and include courses for women's colleges or classes in decoration. There are about one-hundred-eighty pictures in each lecture. Fuller information on request.

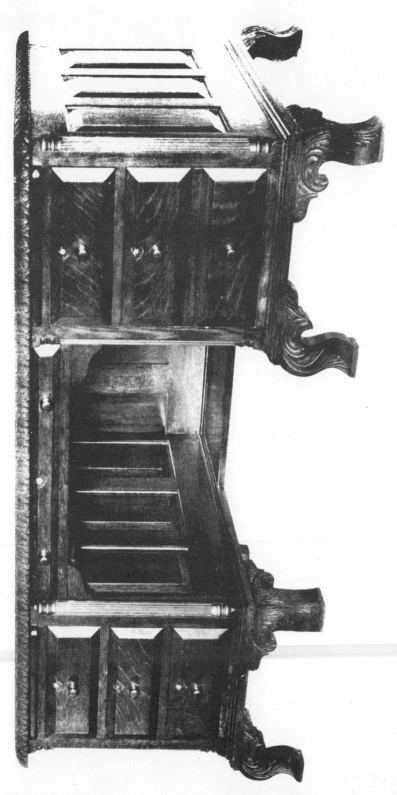

THE PUBLIC ARE HEREBY NOTIFIED THAT THE ABOVE OBJECT AND ALL FOLLOWING FURNITURE IN THE BOOK UNTIL IRON IS REACHED ARE ADAPTATIONS OF THE ANTIQUE AND ARE NOT CORRECT COPIES. THE REASON FOR THIS IS THAT THERE IS A LEGITIMATE DEMAND FOR A FLAT TOP DESK, ONE OF WHICH HAS ALREADY BEEN SHOWN, BUT NO OTHERS, PRACTICAL, ARE KNOWN TO MR. NUTTING. THE ABOVE IS 735C IN OAK. OFFERED ALSO IN MAHOGANY AND WALNUT. 735D, THE SAME, CARVED FEET ONLY

735   FIVE PANEL BACK, 36 X 66. 735A FOUR PANEL BACK, 30 X 60
WALNUT, OAK, MAHOGANY, OR MAPLE

A BEAUTIFUL, DIGNIFIED, SOLID DESK, ADAPTED FROM THE FINEST ANTIQUE
DESIGN. HAND MADE HANDLES. 736   TYPIST'S DESK, 30 X 50

737   ADAPTED CHIPPENDALE, 36 X 66, FIVE PANEL BACK, 30 X 60, FOUR
PANEL BACK. MAPLE, MAHOGANY, OR WALNUT

738   TYPIST'S DESK, 30 X 60, TWO TIERS. 738A   TYPIST'S DESK, 30 X 50
738B   TYPIST'S DESK, ONE TIER

749   DESK ADAPTED FROM CONNECTICUT CHEST PATTERN. OAK,
APPLIED MOLDINGS MAROON, INCISED MOLDINGS AND
CORNER BLOCKS BLACK. 30 X 50 X 30

746   BANK CHECK DESK. MAPLE. 62 X 21¾ X 57

747   OAK CHEST DESK, TOP SOLID OAK, 36 x 66
748   ADAPTED FOR TYPEWRITER

397   STENO. LEATHER SWIVEL   497   SHORT ARM, SWIVEL CHAIR

CHAIRS BUILT ON PENSHURST BASE, VERY RIGID. PIGSKIN AT EXTRA CHARGE

656   TABLE DESK, MAPLE, 40 X 20¼ X 28¼ HIGH
FOUR DRAWERS. USED ALSO AS EARLY DRESSING TABLE. ADAPTED

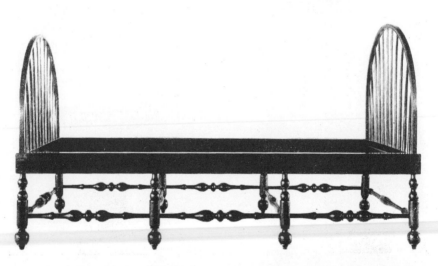

814   MAPLE, HEAD AND FOOT DETACHABLE, HEAD 46 HIGH
THIS PIECE IS ADAPTED. MADE 39 X 82 ONLY

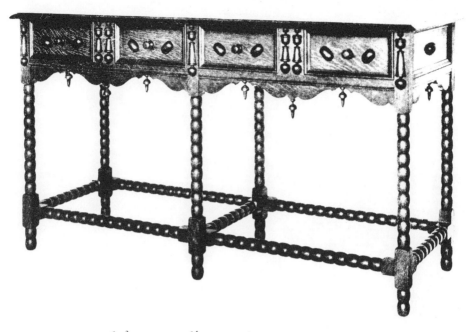

912 OAK, $63\frac{3}{4}$ X 22 X $36\frac{1}{2}$ HIGH. HEIGHT MAY BE INCREASED OR DECREASED. 912A WITHOUT ORNAMENTS

AN EXACT DOUBLING OF THE ONLY OLD AMERICAN SIDEBOARD TABLE KNOWN IN OAK

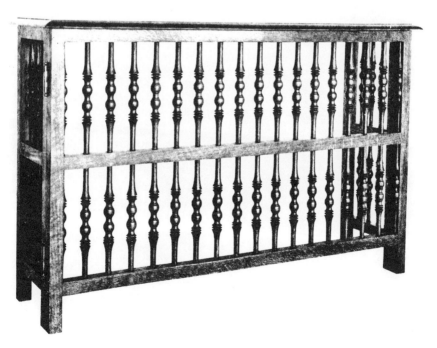

15 RADIATOR MASK, OAK. ANY HEIGHT OR LENGTH. TWO DOORS

A ROOM, LATE 18TH CENTURY WITH OUR FURNISHING

ALL FURNITURE IN THIS ROOM SHOWN BY NUMBER

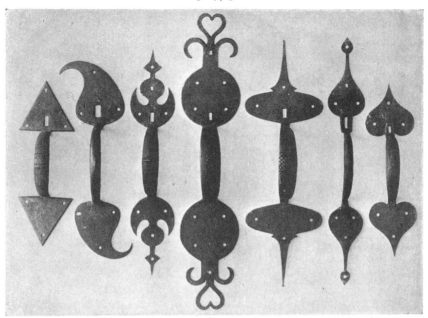

I—I   I—2   I—3   I—4   I—5   I—6   I—7

12 INCH, 14 INCH, 15 INCH, 22 INCH,   16½ INCH, 16½ INCH, 11 INCH

PLATES ONLY ARE SHOWN. ALL LATCHES SUPPLIED WITH FIVE PARTS

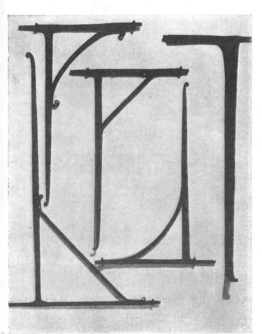

I—263, I—259, I—268, I—269, I—258
36 TO 54 INCHES

I—72   TIN CHANDELIER, SPREAD 23,
HEIGHT 24

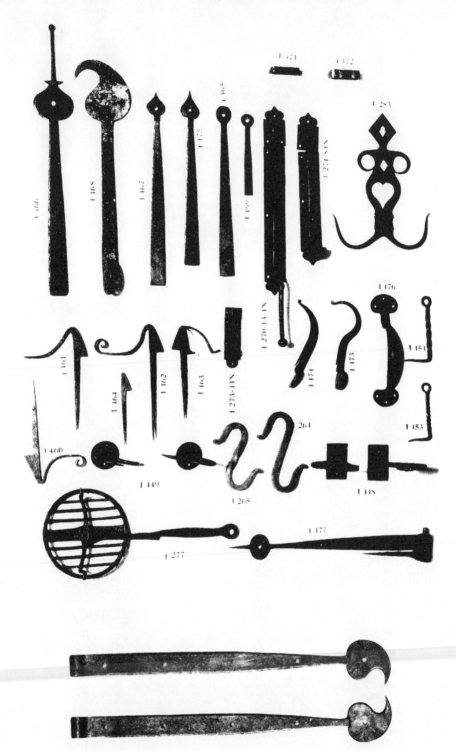

I-40   TULIP BUD HINGE MATCHING LATCH I-2 AND LATCH BAR I-468

I–251 GOOSE HEAD
18 INCHES HIGH

I–249 CONE HEAD
10 INCHES HIGH

THE GOOSE HEAD ANDIRONS ARE THE MOST QUAINT IRON TYPE

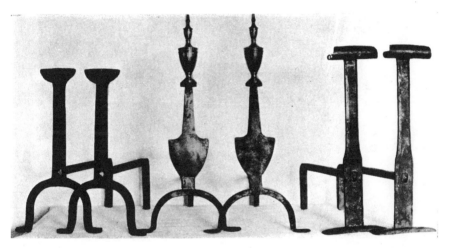

I–255
HEIGHT $16\frac{3}{4}$

I–257
BRASS TIP. $22\frac{1}{2}$ HIGH

I–256
HEIGHT $19\frac{1}{2}$

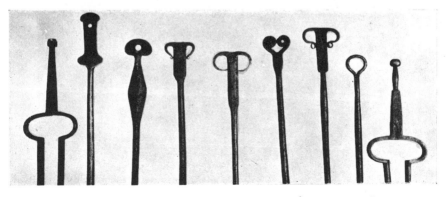

I–240 I–242
    I–243

I–244

I–245

I–246

I–247

I–248
    I–241

I-237   I   LIGHT
I-238   2   LIGHT

ORDERS SHOULD HAVE CAPITAL I PREFIXED TO ALL IRON NUMBERS

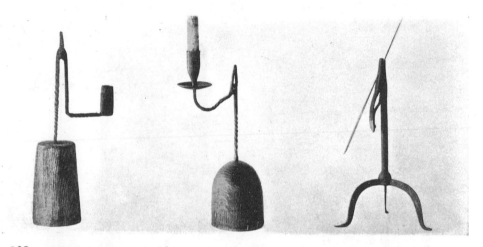

I-120   CRUDE SCONCE   I-121   TURNED BASE SCONCE   I-122   IRON SPRING
CLIP SCONCE

I-282   SKEWER HOLDER
41   TODDY STICK

I-60   TABLE SCONCE, IRON
$20\frac{1}{2}$ HIGH

B-79   OUR SPECIAL, RARE AND IMPORTANT, MOLDED BRASS BOX LOCK.
ATTACHMENTS UNDER PLATE LEAVE SURFACE UNBROKEN.
NOT MADE RIGHTS AND LEFTS, BUT REVERSED IN THE
OLD FASHION. WE ARE THE ONLY MAKERS

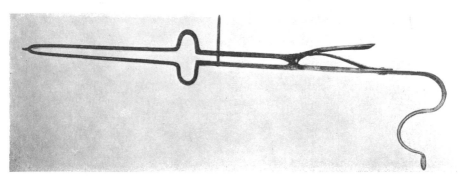

I-223   MOST DELICATE TYPE OF PIPE TONGS. $17\frac{1}{4}$ LONG

I-250   HEART ANDIRONS. $23\frac{1}{2}$ HIGH   I-252   GOOSE NECK AND BALL
PLEASE PLACE CAPITAL I BEFORE NUMBERS OF ALL IRON TO AVOID CONFUSION

I–224   WALL SCONCE, DOUBLE, OF TUBING. MAY BE ELECTRIFIED

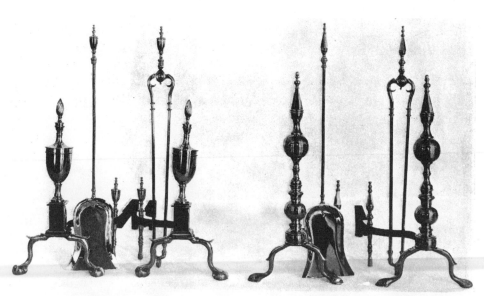

I–262   SPIRAL FLAME, BALL FOOT
       ANDIRONS 18¾ HIGH
I–278   FIRE IRONS TO MATCH

I–260   STEEPLE TOP ANDIRONS
I–276   FIRE IRONS TO MATCH
       ANDIRONS 22 INCHES HIGH

I—15 WISH BONE SPRING LATCH, 7 X 3

I—235A   I—236   I—239A   I—235

I—220   I—221   I—221A   I—221B   I—236

1-164   IRON OR BRASS, ADJUSTABLE
MILLED HEAD. SNUFFERS. 21½ HIGH

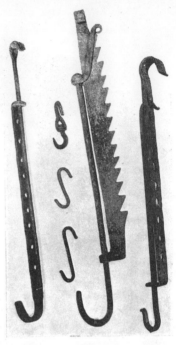

1-287   1-267   1-286
           1-264

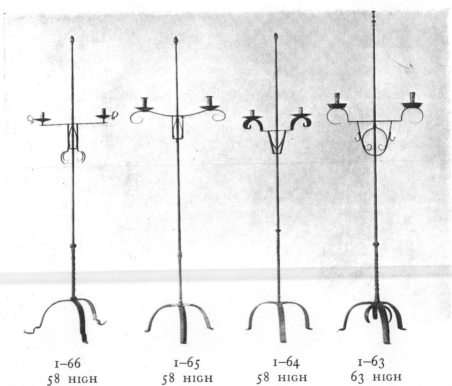

1-66   1-65   1-64   1-63
58 HIGH   58 HIGH   58 HIGH   63 HIGH

B—101   B—102   B—103   TALLEST $8\frac{3}{4}$ HIGH

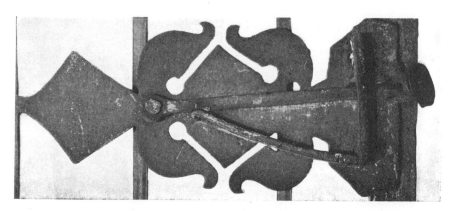

I—470   AN ENGLISH CASEMENT WINDOW LATCH. $9\frac{1}{4}$ LONG. IRON

B—49   LIFTING BRASS, HEAVY, FOR ENDS OF SECRETARIES. $6\frac{1}{2}$ INCHES LONG

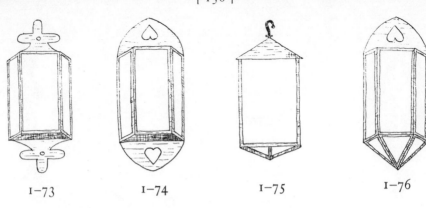

I–73   I–74   I–75   I–76

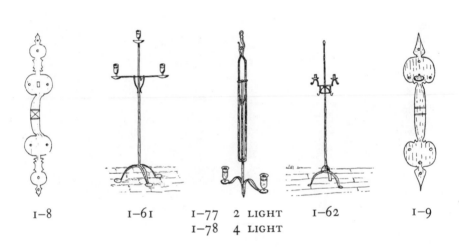

I–8   I–61   I–77   2 LIGHT   I–62   I–9
                       I–78   4 LIGHT

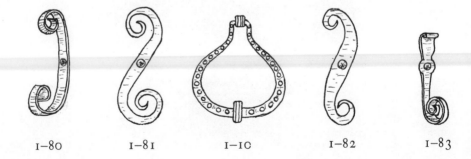

I–80   I–81   I–10   I–82   I–83

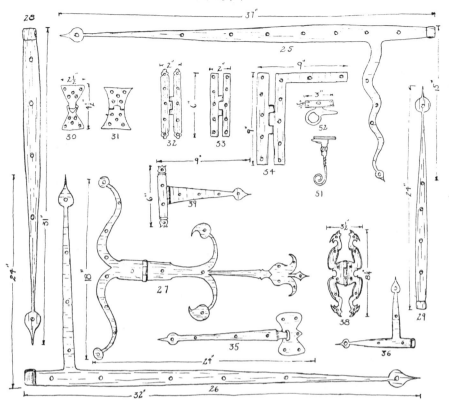

MOST OF THE HINGES ARE MADE IN SIZES TO ORDER AS WELL
AS IN SIZES INDICATED

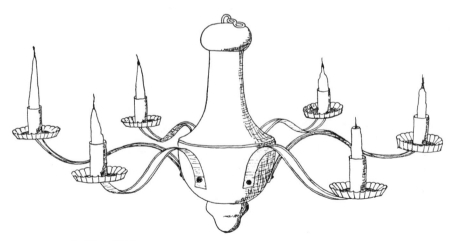

I–71 WOOD HUB CHANDELIER, 29 SPREAD, 11 HIGH
FITTED FOR ELECTRICITY ALSO. ATTACHED TO CEILING
BY CHAIN ANY DESIRED LENGTH
I–71B THE SAME ELECTRIFIED, READY FOR INSTALLATION
IRON OF ANY DEGREE OF SIMPLICITY OR ELABORATION MADE TO ORDER

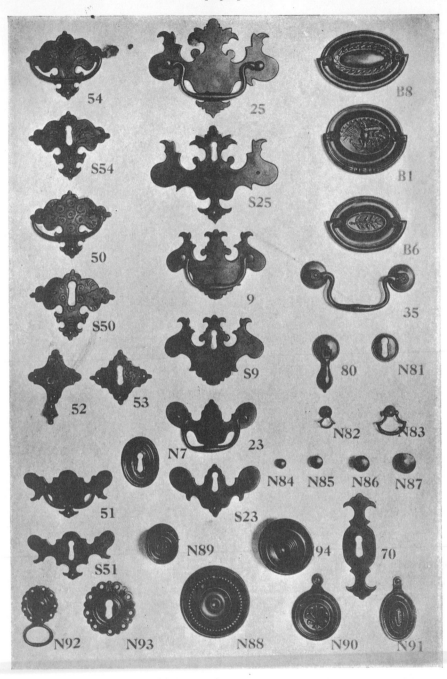

HANDMADE AND FILED BRASSES, CAREFULLY BEVELED EDGES
OTHER SIZES SUPPLIED
ALL MY FURNITURE IS SUPPLIED WITH THESE

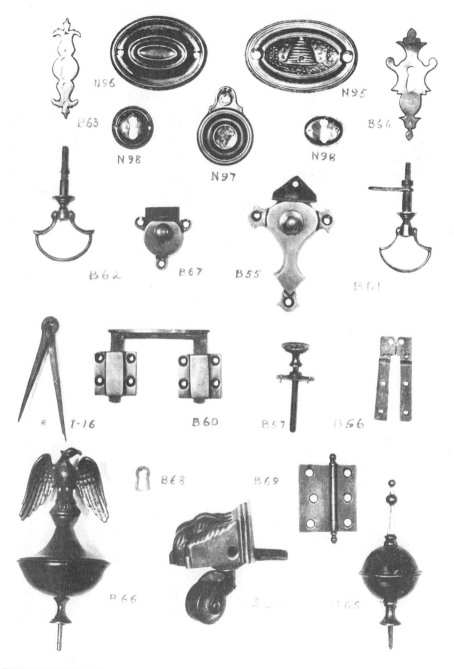

THESE BRASSES ARE MADE FOR US. B—59, NOT SHOWN, IS A SPECIAL PATTERN
OF OUR OWN LIKE B-58 BUT WITH A DOME OF SILENCE, DOING AWAY WITH
THE CASTER. OTHER OBJECTS DESCRIBED IN PRICE LIST. OTHER PATTERNS
AVAILABLE. ORDERS SHOULD HAVE CAPITAL B PREFIXED TO ALL BRASS
NUMBERS IGNORE THE N IN ABOVE NUMBERS

B–73   B–74   B–72   B–71
THE LARGE S KNOCKER IS THE MOST DESIRABLE OLD TYPE

I–279   I–280
TRIVETS ARE NOW CONSIDERED VERY DESIRABLE

PRICE LIST

OF

WALLACE NUTTING
REPRODUCTIONS

WALLACE NUTTING REPRODUCTIONS

FEBRUARY 1, 1932

Small Articles

1	Curly frame, 3⅝″	$1.00
2	Curly frame, 4¾″	1.50
3	Curly frame, 5⅝″	2.00
3A	Shaving glass, curly, 4½″	2.75
3B	Curly frame, glass, 5½″	3.75
3C	Shaving glass, curly, 7¼″	4.50
4	Curly pepper, maple	1.00
5	Sand shaker, curly	2.75
6	Curly ink well	1.25
7	Snuff box, curly	1.75
8	Handy box, curly, 3″	2.50
9	Handy box, curly, 4″	3.00
10	Shot well, curly	1.00
11	Pen tray, curly	2.50
12	Candlestick, 8″	3.50
14	Pedestal tray, mah.	9.00
15	Radiator mask, per ft.	12.00
17	New England tripod stand	13.00
18	Fluted stand	30.00
19	Wafer holder, boxwood	3.00
20	Handy box, curly, 7″	7.50
21	Screw candlestand	36.00
22	Cross base candlestand	18.00
23	Dictionary rest	25.00
24	Costumer	24.00
25	Curly maple cup	1.20
25B	Curly maple goblet	1.80
26	Reversible plate, 8″	3.00
27	Curly maple salt, 2½″	.60
28	Individual salt	.45
29	Curly maple saucer	.80
30	Curly maple plate, 9″	3.60
30B	Curly maple plate, 8″	3.00
31	Low candlestick	1.80
31B	Small candlestick	.75
32	Pole screen, Hepplewhite	36.00
33	Mahogany knife box	9.00
35	Pole screen, mahogany	54.00
36	Carved pole screen	75.00

Finials

34	Big ball finial, 7½″ high	3.00
37	Highboy spiral finial	7.00
38	Chapin, open scroll, 11½″	9.00
39	Low spiral finial, 8¾″	7.00
40	Spinning wheel rack	12.00
41	Large toddy stick	1.00
42	Q. A. walnut finial, 7¼″	1.80
42B	Same, but spiral 7″ high	5.00
43	Clock finial, Pa. 6″ high	5.70
43B	Miniature, for glass	.60
44	Goddard clock finial	7.50
44B	Same, but wider	9.00
45	Clock or highboy finial	6.90
45B	17th c. drop for table	.60
46	Bookcase finial, spiral	6.00
46B	Pine gilded acorn, banjo	4.50
47	Spiral large finial, 6¾″	7.50
48	Spiral urn finial, 6″ high	7.50
48B	Roll edge urn finial, 7¼″	9.00
49	Slender spiral finial, 8″	7.50
49B	Mahogany spiral finial, 7″ high	7.50
50	Goddard highboy finial	13.00
50B	Pine gilded drop, mirror	2.25
51	As 50, but little larger	13.00
51B	Sec. or highboy, odd	7.50
52	Phila. finial, 7½″ high	9.00
52B	Simple Chapin, 7″ high	1.25
53	Largest Pa. chest on ch.	9.90
53B	Maple, crude finial, 8″	6.00
54	Bed finial, 4⅞″ high	1.00
54B	Bed finial, 4¾″ high	1.00
54C	Small bed finial, 5″ high	1.00
54D	Bed finial, 1⅜″ high	1.00
54E	Like 54D, narrower	.75
55	17th c. drop, table, 3¼″	.75
55B	17th c. drop, mirror, 2″	.60
55C	Queen Anne drop, 2¾″	.60
55D	Queen Anne table drop, ¾″ w.	.60
55E	Q. A. drop, miniature	.60
56B	Gilded finial, 3½″ high	4.50
57	Large table finial, 8¼″	2.00
57B	Larger intersection finial	2.00
58	For X intersection, 4½″	2.75
58C	Tambour secretary finial, 4″	1.00

Clocks

59	Willard clock, qu. col.	450.00
59B	Same without qu. col.	425.00
60	Hall clock, mahogany shell	560.00
61	Banjo clock, gold leaf	110.00
62	Gold leaf bracket	20.00
63	Curtis lyre clock	200.00
64	Curtis, mahogany and gold	570.00
65	Hall, block and shell	600.00
66	Same with brass face	625.00
68	Phila. type clock	475.00
68B	Same with added panel	500.00
69	Shelf clock, mahogany	250.00
70	Shelf clock, painted	250.00

76	Largest carved finial..........	22.50
77	Carved foliage, large.........	18.00
78	Reeded lid, narrow frame.....	9.00
79	Carved, with festoons........	90.00
80	Large carved urn, Pa........	30.00
81	Chapin secretary finial........	4.00
82	Chapin, small, deep cut.......	3.00
83	Urn and spike, like brass.....	2.00
84	Ball and spike, like clock.....	2.00
85	Dainty spiral like 46.........	5.70
86	Shelf clock finial, cen........	3.00
87	Thomas Harland finial.......	5.70
88	Thomas Harland, small.......	5.25
89	Tall clock finial, 4¾"........	1.00
90	Pa. tall clock, large..........	9.00
91	Drop for 3-leg stand, 3½"....	6.00
92	Conn. chest on chest, 6"......	2.00
93	Shelf clock finial, 3¼"........	.90
94	Carved pointed finial........	7.50
95	Highboy finial, 8"...........	11.50
96	Drop for lowboy, 3½".......	.60
97	Large hollow urn, 4½".......	6 00
98	Conn. highboy finial..........	5.70

STOOLS

101	Windsor stool, round.........	5.50
102	Windsor stool, oval.........	9.00
103	Milking stool, handle........	2.00
104	Boot jack, fish shape........	3.00
107	Bamboo stool, round........	5.50
110	New England stool, oval......	7.50
127	New England stool, ogee......	10.00
143	Penna. stool, ogee............	15.00
144	Window seat, Sheraton.......	100.00
145	Windsor stool, round.........	13.50
153	Penna. stool, oval............	7.50
155	Penna. stool, ogee...........	7.50
161	Joint stool, splayed, 18"......	24.00
161A	Joint stool, 20"..............	27.00
161B	Joint stool, 22"..............	28.00
161C	Joint stool, 24"...............	29.00
162	Long form, four legs.........	54.00
162B	Short form, four legs........	50.00
163	Long form, six legs..........	70.00
164	Brewster stool, 3 legs........	17.00
165	Low joint stool..............	22.50
166	Rush seat stool, 15" high......	13.00
167	Same, stretchers, 18"........	19.50
168	Same, stretchers, 22"........	21.00
169	Same, stretchers, 29"........	24.00
170	Jacobean stool, 20" long.....	27.00
171	Jacobean stool, 30" long.....	32.00
173	Pine trestle stool............	37.50
174	Dutch walnut stool..........	54.00
174B	Same, with carved knee.......	59.00
175	Tavern sign, lettered........	36.00
175B	with stage coach...........	52.00

176	Tavern sign, oval, large.......	52.00
176B	with stage coach...........	70.00
177	Simple light sign............	24.00
178	Elaborate sign, large........	80.00
178B	with painted design........	100.00
179	Chippendale stool	66.00
179B	Same, carved hip.'...........	88.00
180	Chippendale stool	42.00
204	Baby's slat back chair........	24.00
209	Penna. high chair............	48.00
210	Windsor high chair...........	42.00
211	Baby's low comb back........	24.00
290	Maple bench, 6 legs..........	42.00
292	Gothic stool	6.60

SIDE CHAIRS

301	Bow back braced Win........	29.00
302	Bow back, no brace..........	25.00
305	Bent rung bamboo...........	30.00
309	Fan back, no brace...........	25.00
310	Windsor, no brace...........	25.00
311	Windsor imposed comb.......	36.00
325	Like 525, Chippendale........	150.00
325B	Like 525, but Q. A...........	120.00
326	Fan braced Windsor..........	29.00
326B	Same, curly maple..........	36.00
329	Windsor swivel chair.........	42.00
333	Windsor comb back..........	33.00
334	Chip. carved, fluted.........	180.00
335	Sheraton, carved	120.00
337	Hep. John Goddard..........	135.00
338	Hep. tied reed back..........	135.00
338B	Hep. no carving.............	90.00
341	Hep. three feather...........	147.00
342	Hep. five reed back..........	135.00
342B	Same, not carved............	100.00
343	Chip. richest type............	300.00
349	Slipper chair, Windsor.......	26.00
355	Windsor high desk chair......	31.00
356	Chip. side, mahogany........	150.00
358	Chip. carved, fluted.........	130.00
359	Chip. four ladder back.......	135.00
359B	Chip. carved ladders........	130.00
360	Cromwellian, leather	78.00
360B	Same, grain leather	63.00
361	Dutch turned, rushed........	29.00
362	Chip. three ladders..........	75.00
363	Chip. ribbon back...........	75.00
363B	Same, fully carved...........	80.00
364	Carver side, rushed..........	40.00
365	Light wild rose chair........	36.00
369	Chip. French scroll..........	195.00
371	Hep. shield back.............	150.00
375	Span. foot fiddle back........	54.00
375B	Same as 375, turned foot......	51.00
375C	Same, carved back..........	57.00
376	Flemish, carved	240.00
377	Three slat back, new........	27.00

380	Span. foot, baluster..........	69.00
390	New England five back.......	45.00
391	Penna. six back, rushed.......	48.00
392	Light four back..............	36.00
392B	Same, curly maple...........	42.00
393	Pilgrim three back...........	33.00
394	Leather chair, carved.........	81.00
397	Stenographer's swivel chair....	81.00
398	Watnut Dutch chair..........	99.00
399	Q. A. scrolled posts..........	147.00
399C	Ball foot, carved knee........	240.00

Arm Chairs

401	New England Windsor arm...	40.50
402	New England comb back......	45.00
404	Baby's high chair............	33.00
405	Bent rung bamboo...........	36.00
406	Wainscot chair	90.00
407	Light comb back, Windsor....	57.00
408	Light bow back, carved.......	49.50
411	Great Brewster chair.........	75.00
412	Great Penna. comb back......	57.00
413	Penna. low back, Windsor.....	45.00
413B	Same, smaller size...........	36.00
415	Flare comb back.............	59.00
415B	Same, curly back and base.....	66.00
416	Pine wing chair, panel.......	42.00
420	Bow back, knuckle arm.......	57.00
421	Imposed comb, knuckle.......	63.00
422	Tenoned fan back, brace......	57.00
425	Arm chair like 525...........	190.00
425B	Same, Queen Anne type.......	150.00
427	Bamboo bent rung...........	42.00
427B	Same, straight rung..........	39.00
430	Roundabout chair, rush.......	45.00
434	Chip. fluted posts............	240.00
436	Sheraton easy chair..........	240.00
437	Hep. John Goddard..........	168.00
438	Hep. tied reed back..........	169.00
438B	Hep. not carved.............	135.00
440	Penna. writing arm..........	98.00
442	Five reed back..............	162.00
442B	Same, no carving............	138.00
443	Chippendale, engrailed	300.00
451	Taper turned writing.........	90.00
452	Sheraton Martha Washington..	200.00
456	Chip. carved, b. and c........	180.00
456B	Same, carved knee...........	195.00
458	Chip. fluted leg.............	160.00
459	Chip. four ladders...........	156.00
459B	Four ladder back............	150.00
460	Cromwellian leather	90.00
461	Simple Dutch, rushed........	39.00
462	Chip. three ladders..........	110.00
463	Chip. straight leg...........	110.00
463B	Same, ribbon back, c.........	115.00
464	Carver chair, rushed.........	60.00
465	Walnut wing chair...........	210.00

465B	Wild rose, balusters..........	45.00
466	Chip. wing, stretchers.......	231.00
468	Chip. wing, straight leg......	141.00
468B	Same, stretchers.............	153.00
469	Chip. French scroll..........	240.00
470	Five slat rocking............	48.00
471	Hep. shield back, mahogany...	195.00
473	Chip. Martha Washington....	135.00
474	Cane arm chair..............	150.00
475	Span. foot, fiddle back.......	78.00
475B	Same, turned foot...........	72.00
476	Flemish, carved	180.00
476B	Same. carved panel..........	270.00
480	Spanish foot, baluster........	105.00
481	Leather easy chair...........	168.00
490	New England five back.......	66.00
491	Penna. six back, rushed......	66.00
492	New England four back......	48.00
493	Pilgrim three back..........	63.00
493B	Lighter Pilgrim arm.........	57.00
494	Carved leather, walnut.......	126.00
495	Tip and turn leather........	120.00
496	Chip. roundabout	140.00
496B	Same, carved knee..........	150.00
498	Dutch, plain saddle.........	132.00
499	Queen Anne, scrolled........	192.00
499C	Ball foot, carved knee........	270.00

Settles, Settees, Etc.

513	Pine settle, three panel.......	84.00
513B	Two panel back.............	72.00
514	New England ten legger......	162.00
515	Triple back, ten leg.........	195.00
525	Chip. six leg sofa...........	594.00
525B	Same, four legs..............	420.00
533	Penna. ten legger...........	162.00
534	Chip. short settee...........	450.00
534B	Same, three back............	600.00
538	Hep. wheat ear settee........	450.00
539	Sheraton sofa, 22 x 82........	465.00
545	Penna. settee, ten leg........	168.00
552	Sheraton love seat...........	294.00
556	Chip. three chair back........	594.00
559	Four ladder back............	594.00
559B	Same, not carved............	450.00
560	Jacobean sofa, leather........	420.00
560B	Same, pigskin	450.00
564	New England love seat.......	90.00
565	Comb back love seat.........	111.00
568B	Chip. sofa like 468B..........	450.00
569	Chip. French foot...........	600.00
574	Flemish couch, carved.......	300.00
579	Sheraton settee	495.00
589	Wainscot settle	186.00
590	Five back, six leg............	110.00
591	Three chair back.............	150.00
594	Comb back, ten legger.......	180.00
595	Comb back, eight leg........	145.00

598	Walnut settee, three	430.00
599	Dutch, three back	525.00
599B	Three carved back	660.00

TABLES, STANDS

601	Heavy refectory table	144.00
601B	Heavy refectory, mid. str.	144.00
602	Heavy refectory, carved	240.00
603	Drop leaf, splayed	105.00
604	Dutch porringer table	59.00
605	Three leg Windsor	17.00
606	Hep. high stand	32.00
607	Oak refectory, six legs	240.00
607B	Same, carved (as 602)	444.00
607C	Same, 36 x 156	510.00
608	Two. dr., maple or mahogany	66.00
608C	Same, curly maple	72.00
609	Pine top trestle,, 30 w	93.00
609B	Pine trestle, 36 x 72	99.00
609C	Same, 30 x 60	72.00
610	Oak trestle, 36 x 72	117.00
610B	Oak, 36 x 84 (pine 115)	120.00
610C	Pine, 36 x 96	129.00
611	Pine trestle, 30 x 108	117.00
611B	Pine, 36 x 108	126.00
612	Pine, 36 x 120	144.00
612B	Pine, 36 x 132	147.00
613	Ball turned tavern	72.00
614	Pine trestle table	36.00
614B	Pine trestle, 40" long	45.00
615	Pine trestle, 30 x 50	72.00
615B	Oak trestle, 30 x 60	81.00
615C	Same, pine	75.00
616	Single folding gate	42.00
617	Swedish vase trestle	105.00
618	Knoll trestle oak, 108"	330.00
618B	Same, 41 x 96	291.00
618C	Same, 14 ft.	570.00
619	Crane bracket table	114.00
620	Span. foot gate, 48 x 59	180.00
621	Four gate, 48 x 59	180.00
622	Four gate, 60 x 70	221.00
622B	Spanish foot gate	312.00
623	Butterfly, 28 x 36	57.00
624	Butterfly, 30 x 40	69.00
625	Trestle butterfly	49.00
626	Trumpet, X stretcher	111.00
627	Lazy Susan	99.00
627B	Same, carved	170.00
628	Pembroke, mahogany, 36" sq.	96.00
628B	Pembroke, vertical stretcher	105.00
629	Pembroke, Hep. maple	57.00
629B	Same, inlaid, mahogany	90.00
630	Chip. torchere, b. and c.	72.00
631	Two gate, 60 x 70	210.00
632	Plain two gate, 48 x 59	135.00
633	Hep. stand, octagon	27.00
634	Chip. card, b. and c.	276.00

635	Pembroke, Chip., fine	138.00
636	Heavy four gate	400.00
636B	Heavy four gate, walnut	420.00
637	Maple library table	108.00
637B	Same, walnut	111.00
638	Library, oak, six leg	450.00
639	Bedside stand, four leg	48.00
640	Mahogany library, b. and c.	249.00
640B	Same, carved	375.00
641	Sideboard, arched	327.00
641B	Dressing table	321.00
642	Mahogany Chip. half (659)	90.00
642B	Square leaf table	114.00
643	Sheraton four leg stand	54.00
643B	Curly and mahogany	60.00
644	Hep. tripod, inlaid	66.00
646	Hep. mahogany tip, oval	39.00
647	Dutch round, dished	42.00
647B	Same, dished, tip, 24" high	39.00
647C	Same, plain top	33.00
648	Dutch round, dining	117.00
648B	Chippendale, b. and c.	144.00
649	Mahogany serving, drawer	129.00
650	Chippendale hall or side	750.00
650B	Carved legs only	345.00
653	Turned, splayed	42.00
654	Pine hutch table	36.00
655	High stretcher tavern	90.00
656	Dressing, adapted	135.00
658	Mahogany card, fluted	174.00
659	Mahogany fluted, square	117.00
660	Tavern table, drawer	63.00
661	Hep. card, inlaid	150.00
662	Coffee table, pine top	28.50
663	Carved foot piecrust	66.00
664	Same, all carved	78.00
665	Chip. mahogany sideboard	270.00
665B	Gadroon, sideboard	315.00
665C	Fully carved	480.00
667	Dutch sideboard	270.00
668	Sheraton card table	150.00
669	Small dressing, plain	66.00
669B	Same, reeded, mahogany	72.00
670	Hep. three part, inlaid	390.00
671	Center only, inlaid	171.00
672	End only, inlaid	114.00
673	Sheraton three part	375.00
674	Center only	171.00
675	End only	114.00
676	Sheraton two part	294.00
678	Arched dressing table	135.00
680	Three part, Chippendale	570.00
680B	Dutch dining, three part	476.00
681	Three part, Phyfe	474.00
681B	Same, plain	456.00
682	Sheraton sideboard	600.00
682B	Same, carved	650.00
683	Hep. sideboard, plain	420.00
683B	Same, veneered	759.00

683c	Same, small, plain	285.00
684	Drop leaf, Phyfe	234.00
684b	Same, no carving	153.00
685	Plain Hep. serving	72.00
689	Lowboy like 989	252.00
691	Maple lowboy (mahogany 186)	180.00
692	Mahogany lowboy	450.00
693	Chippendale piecrust	270.00
693b	Same, fully carved	369.00
694	Dutch tea, dished	162.00
695	Curly tray top	145.00
696	Curly Dutch, 18"	36.00
696b	Curly tray top	39.00
697	Walnut card table	120.00
698	Dutch serving, walnut	177.00
699	Walnut lowboy, W. and M.	222.00
699b	Veneered lowboy	360.00

Desks

700	Small oak, no drawer	84.00
700b	Small oak, drawer, new	115.00
701	Large turned, stretcher	205.00
701b	Large turned, walnut	208.00
703	Curly and mahogany tambour	456.00
703b	Tambour desk, mahogany	456.00
703c	Tambour secretary	840.00
704	Secretary (Milton)	900.00
706	Cabriole, Dutch foot	330.00
707	Small mahogany desk, drawer	162.00
707b	Same, without drawer	156.00
710	Washington desk	512.00
716	Walnut ball foot	442.00
717	Walnut ball foot secretary	590.00
726	Trumpet turned, plain	180.00
727	Trumpet turned, curly	250.00
729	Mahogany, fine cabinet	330.00
730	Maple, fine cabinet	315.00
730b	Curly, good cabinet	330.00
731	Maple secretary, square top	450.00
731b	Same, curly maple	594.00
732	Maple secretary, scroll top	590.00
733	All block, supreme	1800.00
734	Lower part only	1000.00
735	Flat top, ogee, mahogany	450.00
735b	Smaller, eight panel	420.00
735c	Any wood, carved	750.00
735d	Same, plain top	525.00
736	Typist, like 735	300.00
737	Chippendale, adapted	400.00
738	Typist, like 737	300.00
738b	Single typist	220.00
739	Ox bow, ball and claw	405.00
739b	Same, bracket foot	295.00
740	Ox bow, secretary bracket	594.00
745	Flat top, turned	615.00
746	Standing check desk	135.00
747	Oak, flat, chest style	420.00
747b	Same, 30 x 60	390.00
748	Same, typewriter	270.00
749	Same, single tier	240.00

Mirrors

750	Elizabethan, carved	60.00
751	Heavy walnut mirror	69.00
753	Mantel, gold	300.00
754	Chip., maple or mahogany	36.00
755	Walnut with picture	72.00
756	Same, two glasses	72.00
757	Richest Georgian	450.00
758	Empire, mantel, curly	90.00
758b	Same, without balls	60.00
760	Q. A., curly or mahogany	72.00
761	Three feather, mahogany	42.00
762	Pine, carved	54.00
762b	Same, gilded	72.00
763	Walnut, carved, gold	63.00
764	Carved bird	72.00
765	Chip. mahogany, gold bird	115.00
766	Chip. mantel, scrolled	75.00
767	Courting mirror, small	51.00
768	Simple, Q. A., small	10.00
769	Hep. filigree	294.00
770	Curly or mahogany shaving	69.00
771	Hepplewhite, shaving	48.00
772	Plain, small	12.00
773	Love bird	72.00
774	Small, simple scroll	18.00
775	Large courting	90.00
776	Georgian, medium	394.00
777	Sher. balls, gilded	75.00
777b	Same, mahogany	37.50

Beds

801	Uph. box spring, 39 x 82	48.00
810b	Single mattress	66.00
802	Uph. spring, 54 x 82	54.00
802b	Mattress, 54 x 82	90.00
803	Uph. spring, 60 x 82	57.00
803b	Mattress, 60 x 82	102.00
804	Choice live goose pillow	6.00
804b	Same, 22 x 28	7.20
805	Feather and down	7.50
805	Same, 22 x 28	9.00
805b	Best feather and down	9.00
805b	Same, 22 x 28	11.40
806	Mahogany bed, carved knee	360.00
806b	Four carved posts	450.00
807	Urn top bed, medium	54.00
808	Hired man's bed, acorn	51.00
809	Low post bed, urn top	49.00
809b	Head and foot same	51.00
810	Walnut Dutch crib	114.00
811	Oak Brewster bed	120.00
812	Carved and turned	183.00
813	Heavy, turned foot	114.00
815	Maple, fluted, turned	120.00

817	Flat top canopy frame........	15.00
818	Ogee tester frame only.......	19.00
818B	Pointed ogee tester...........	21.00
819	Plain oval tester.............	21.00
820	Rounded top frame..........	21.00
821	Hep. taper feet, light.........	99.00
821B	Hep. reeded, light...........	112.00
821C	Same, mahogany	115.00
822	Chippendale plain, fluted.....	90.00
823	Mahogany, two posts carved...	195.00
823B	Four posts carved............	213.00
824	Chaise longue, b. and c.......	330.00
825	Penna. daybed, rushed........	135.00
826	Sheraton carved, mahogany....	300.00
826B	Same, half high.............	231.00
827	Maple fluted, r. mold........	180.00
828	Chaise longue, maple or mah...	225.00
829	Dutch chaise longue.........	240.00
831	Pilgrim post, foot rail.......	108.00
832	Two carved posts............	180.00
832B	Four carved posts............	249.00
835	Light daybed, turned.........	207.00
836	Sheraton light, mahogany.....	78.00
836B	Same, curly, turned..........	93.00
836C	Plain maple	66.00
837	Sheraton, reeded, light........	96.00
839	Half high, turned feet........	78.00
839B	Same, small	57.00
840	Two carved posts, mahogany...	330.00
840B	Same, four carved posts.......	420.00
841	Two carved posts, mahogany..	330.00
841B	Same, four carved posts.......	426.00
842	Half high, foot rail..........	72.00
843	Curly bed, canopy frame......	195.00
844	Curly bed, no canopy.........	174.00
845	Q. A. two shaped posts.......	174.00
845B	Four shaped posts............	204.00
845C	Same, shell on two posts......	195.00
846	Maple urn turned............	99.00
	curly	108.00
846B	Same, reeded posts...........	115.00
847	Very light, acorn top.........	60.00
847B	Same, low posts..............	54.00
848	Hep. reeded, taper...........	108.00
848B	Same, mahogany	115.00
850	Like F. T. 7504-5............	330.00
850B	Fully carved	450.00

CABINET PIECES

900	Carved oak box..............	66.00
901	Hadley box, initialed.........	69.00
903	Carved spoon rack...........	27.00
905	Scalloped pipe box...........	30.00

906	Pine shelves, open back.......	15.00
907	Pine shelves, back............	37.50
909	One drawer oak chest........	195.00
910	Oak Sudbury cupboard.......	645.00
911	Oak court cupboard..........	720.00
912	Oak sideboard, six leg........	234.00
912B	Same, no ornaments..........	210.00
915	Pine chest of drawers........	99.00
915B	Curly, dovetailed	210.00
916	Maple chest of drawers.......	148.00
916B	Same, curly	195.00
917	Same, mahogany	153.00
918	Plain block front............	265.00
919	Mah. oxbow chest of drawers..	261.00
919B	Same, bracket foot...........	251.00
920	Oak chest on frame..........	150.00
921	Maple chest on chest.........	288.00
922	Oak Welsh dresser...........	300.00
923	Pine dresser, scrolled.........	78.00
924	Simple chest of drawers......	96.00
924B	Same, curly top and drawers...	111.00
925	Pine corner cupboard.........	480.00
926	Hanging cupboard	54.00
927	Pine bookcase-dresser	78.00
928	Same, wider, coved top.......	129.00
929B	Pine cupboard, arched........	66.00
930	Name chest, not lined........	78.00
931	Connecticut sunflower chest....	375.00
933	Norman tooth chest..........	246.00
934	Sheraton ch. of drs., inlaid....	297.00
934B	Same, line inlay.............	198.00
935	Hadley chest, carved.........	375.00
936	Oak chest of drawers.........	240.00
937	Oak chest of drawers, inlaid...	258.00
938	Painted Penna. chest.........	294.00
939	Chippendale Chinese lantern...	90.00
940	Mahogany corner cupboard....	219.00
941	Mahogany ch. of drs., qu. col...	240.00
942	New England pine dresser.....	198.00
943	Pine hanging cupboard.......	27.00
944	Open scroll cupboard.........	78.00
945	Fluted pine cupboard.........	180.00
945B	Same, arched door...........	228.00
947	Scrolled pine dresser.........	285.00
952	Bureau table, knee hole.......	534.00
979	Chest of drawers, bl. and shell.	375.00
980	Sheraton cupboard	450.00
989	Mahogany highboy, flames....	600.00
991	Maple highboy, sunrise.......	375.00
992	Savery highboy, carved.......	1230.00
996	Maple highboy, bonnet.......	610.00
999	Walnut highboy	480.00
999B	Same, veneered	720.00
1000	Chest on chest..............	990.00